Pelican Book A799
SOUTH-EAST ASIA IN TURMOIL

Brian Crozier, who is forty-nine, is chairman of
Forum World Features, London, and divides his
time between journalism and authorship. He resigned
from the *Economist* in 1964 after nearly ten years as
that paper's expert on South-East Asia and the Far
East, and the Editor of a confidential bulletin on
world affairs with an influential readership all over
the world. He has been a regular broadcaster on the
B.B.C.'s General Overseas and French and Spanish
services. A frequent lecturer on South-East Asia and
other subjects at the School of Oriental and African
Studies, St Anthony's College, Oxford, Chatham
House, and other institutions, he toured the United
States lecturing in 1961. As a foreign correspondent
he has interviewed many of the leaders of the new
countries, including the late President Ngo Dinh
Diem of South Vietnam, Ho Chi Minh of North
Vietnam, Prince Sihanouk of Cambodia, and Prince
Souvanna Phouma of Laos.

Brian Crozier was stationed in South-East Asia in
1952-3, first as Reuter's correspondent and later with
the *Straits Times* and the *New York Times*. He is the
author of *The Rebels: a study of post-war insurrections*
(1960), *The Morning After: a study of independence*
(1963), *The Struggle for the Third World* (1966), and
Franco (1967).

SOUTH-EAST ASIA IN TURMOIL

Brian Crozier

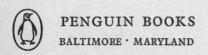

PENGUIN BOOKS
BALTIMORE · MARYLAND

Penguin Books Ltd, Harmondsworth,
Middlesex, England
Penguin Books Inc., 7110 Ambassador Court,
Baltimore, Maryland 21207, U.S.A.
Penguin Books Australia Ltd, Ringwood,
Victoria, Australia

First published 1965
Revised and reprinted in Pelican Books 1966
Revised edition 1968
Copyright © Brian Crozier, 1965, 1968

Made and printed in Great Britain by
Cox & Wyman Ltd, London, Reading and Fakenham
Set in Monotype Plantin

CONTENTS

Contents

FOREWORD

Witnesses in British courts of justice are required to swear that they will tell the truth, the whole truth, and nothing but the truth. I do not claim as much for this book: to have told the whole truth would have made it too massive for its purpose. I have condensed the historical background, preserving what seemed to me relevant to present troubles. What is left is, as far as it lies within my capacity, 'nothing but the truth'.

It is no use pretending this has been easy. To give one instance, an American, Mr William J. Pomeroy, who helped the Filipino Huks, was gaoled with their leaders and now lives in London, disputes the version of events that appears on page 68. The Philippine Communist Party was not, he says, divided into 'Russian' and 'Chinese' wings; but it *was* divided over the tactics to adopt towards Osmeña. According to Pomeroy, it was Vicente Lava who favoured supporting Osmeña, while a Filipino known as 'Jerry' wanted the party to boycott the 1946 elections. As for Pedro Castro, says Pomeroy, he had no strong feelings one way or the other; and nobody wanted a showdown. Mr Pomeroy, of course, was there and I was not. He may be right; or he may have his reasons for presenting his own version of the facts. All I can do is record his dissent. I have indicated other conflicting versions of facts or events in footnotes.

This, then, is not a contemporary history of South-East Asia, but an inquiry into the origins and causes of current turbulence in that area, and a modest attempt to find out what can and cannot be done about it.

BRIAN CROZIER

1941. May: Ho Chi Minh (Vietnam) sets up Viet Minh front.

1942. 15 February: Fall of Singapore.

1943. August: Japanese sponsor 'independent' Burma government.

September: Japanese sponsor 'independent' Philippine Republic.

1945. March: Japanese overpower Vichy garrisons in Indo-China; Emperor Bao Dai made to proclaim Vietnam's independence.

15 August: Japan surrenders.

17 August: Indonesian nationalists proclaim independence.

2 September: Ho Chi Minh proclaims Vietnam Democratic Republic (Communist).

5 September: Mountbatten's forces reach Singapore.

1946. 7 January: *Modus vivendi* agreement between France and Cambodia.

4 July: Independence of Philippines.

17 August: Franco–Laotian *modus vivendi*.

19 December: Viet Minh attack French (first Indo-China war begins).

1947. 19 July: Aung San of Burma assassinated with most of his cabinet.

17 October: Attlee–Nu Treaty on Burma's independence.

1948. 4 January: Independence of Burma.

7 January: *Renville* truce agreement between Dutch and Indonesian Republicans.

February: Communist-sponsored World Youth Conference in Calcutta, leading to insurrections in Burma (March), the Philippines (April), Malaya (June), and Indonesia (September).

1949. 8 March: French agreement with Bao Dai (Vietnam).

19 July: Laos independent 'within French Union'.

1 October: Chinese People's Republic (Communist) proclaimed.

6 November: Cambodia independent 'within French Union'.

27 December: Dutch transfer sovereignty to Indonesia.

1950. 8 May: American economic and military aid made available to Vietnam, Cambodia, and Laos.

1–17 October: General Giap seizes French border forts in Tonking.

1951. February: Vietnamese Communists launch Lao Dong (workers') party.

1953. April: Viet Minh army invades Laos; Prince Souphannouvong proclaims Pathet Lao administration.

22 October: France recognizes Laotian sovereignty.

9 November: France transfers military powers to Cambodia.

1954. 29 April: Far Eastern conference opens at Geneva.

6 May: Viet Minh launch final assault on Dien Bien Phu.

4 June: France recognizes Vietnam's independence.

19 June: Ngo Dinh Diem becomes Prime Minister of Vietnam.

20–21 July: Geneva agreements on Indo-China: Vietnam partitioned.

8 September: South-East Asia Collective Defence Treaty (SEATO) signed in Manila.

17 September: Luis Taruc, Communist leader of Huk rebels, surrenders in Philippines.

1955. April: Afro-Asian conference at Bandung.

23 October: Diem deposes·Bao Dai by referendum.

1957. 31 August: Independence of Malaya.

November: Agreement between Laotian government and Pathet Lao (Communists).

1958. January: Murders of South Vietnam officials (second Indo-China war begins).

15 February: Indonesian rebel 'government' proclaimed.

27 September: General Ne Win takes over in Burma.

1959. 22 April: Sukarno announces 'guided democracy' for Indonesia.

3 June: Singapore becomes self-governing State within Commonwealth.

4 September: Laos appeals to Security Council, alleging attacks from North Vietnam.

1960. February: Burma returns to parliamentary rule.

9 August: Kong Lae seizes power in Laos.

17 August: Prince Souvanna Phouma forms neutralist government.

10 September: Lao Dong (Communist) resolution on 'liberation' of South Vietnam.

December: Prince Souvanna's government ousted by Laotian right-wingers, Prince Boun Oum forms government.

1961. January: Communists set up National Front for Liberation of South Vietnam.

16 May: International conference on Laos at Geneva.

27 May: Tunku Abdul Rahman launches Malaysia plan.

1962. 8 February: United States Command set up in Vietnam.

2 March: General Ne Win sets up military rule in Burma.

23 June: Prince Souvanna Phouma's coalition government takes office in Laos.

23 July: Geneva conference agreement on Laos.

15 August: Dutch and Indonesians agree on West New Guinea.

1963. February: Indonesia decides to oppose Malaysian project.

9 July: London agreement on Malaysia.

14 September: U Thant mission's report on Malaysia published.

16 September: Malaysia proclaimed.

1 November: Diem overthrown in Vietnam.

5 August: U.S. aircraft bomb North Vietnamese bases.

2 September: Indonesian paratroops land in Malaya.

1965. 6 February: Kosygin visits Hanoi.

7 February: Vietcong attacks U.S. base; Americans start air raids on North Vietnam.

7 April: President Johnson offers unconditional talks on Vietnam.

9 August: Singapore secedes from Malaysia.

30 September: Abortive Communist-backed coup in Indonesia.

December: 'Thailand Patriotic Front' announced from Peking.

1966. 8 February: Honolulu Declaration on Vietnam.

11 August: Indonesia-Malaysia agreement to end 'confrontation'.

23–25 October: Manila summit on Vietnam.

1967. 12 March: Sukarno loses mandate as President: Suharto Acting President.

19–21 March: Johnson and Ky meet in Guam.

7 August: New Association of South-East Asian Nations (ASEAN) formed.

30 August: Indonesia and Malaysia resume diplomatic relations.

3 September: Presidential and Senate elections in South Vietnam.

10 October: Sino-Indonesian diplomatic relations suspended.

22 October: Lower House elections in South Vietnam.

1968. 31 January: Viet Cong offensive launched.

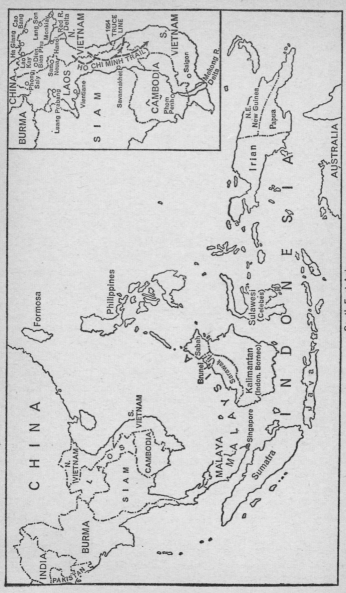

South-East Asia

Inset map (top left):

BURMA
CHINA
Ha Giang · Cao Bang
Lao · Lang Son
Phong · Kay · O'Dien · Red R.
Saly' · Neua · Hanoi · N. Delta
Luang Prabang
LAOS
N. VIETNAM
1954 TRUCE LINE
Vientiane
S I A M
Savannakhet
HO CHI MINH TRAIL
CAMBODIA
Phom Penho
S. VIETNAM
Saigon
Mekong R. Delta

Main map:

C H I N A
INDIA
PAKISTAN
BURMA
N. VIETNAM
S I A M
LAOS
S. VIETNAM
CAMBODIA
Formosa
Philippines
MALAYA
Singapore
M A L A Y S I A
Brunei (Sabah)
Sarawak
Kalimantan (Indon. Borneo)
Sumatra
I N D O N E S I A
Java
Sulawesi (Celebes)
Irian
N.E. New Guinea
Papua
AUSTRALIA

Violence has been the daily fare in various parts of South-East Asia ever since the Japanese armies moved south in 1941. Terrorists have tortured 'traitors' and murdered officials. Insurgents have risen in the name of Nationalism, Communism, or Anti-Communism, and in some places for the spoils of banditry. Old empires have been overthrown and new ones are on the make. There have been revolutions and counter-revolutions, the label depending, often as not, on which side of the iron or bamboo curtain the onlooker is. Great powers have been involved in major wars, directly or by proxy. Colonialism has been the enemy, and more recently, that political curiosity known as 'neo-colonialism'. Aid programmes have been launched to prop up or undermine this régime or that, and much of the cash has found its way into the pockets of corrupt officials. And the price of violence has been the squandering or drying up at source of South-East Asia's prodigious wealth, while millions of new mouths have clamoured for food and low living standards have been further eroded.

There were few relieving touches in this dismal picture. Siam* was occupied by Japan during the Second World War,

* This is Thailand's former name. I have used it throughout this book because there is no mistake about who the Siamese are, whereas the term 'Thais' can refer not only to the inhabitants of Thailand but to related peoples in neighbouring countries as well.

13

but remained on the whole an oasis of peace in South-East Asia until a communist campaign of murder and subversion began in 1965. In Malaya and Singapore, living standards have remained comparatively high, despite a murderous Communist insurrection; and it was not until the autumn of 1963, when Indonesian hostility diverted trade from Singapore and forced new defence burdens on the Federation of Malaysia (to which Singapore at first belonged), that economic strain began to affect the ordinary people of both territories. The Philippines, too, have made progress since independence came in 1946. But these are exceptions. On the whole, conditions have been bad and are getting worse. Burma has been plagued by insurgency ever since independence, and by bad government for most of that period. Chaos and mismanagement were Indonesia's lot under President Sukarno. Vietnam has not known real peace since 1941. The long war against the French ended in 1954, but a few years later the war began again: it was almost the same war, with the Americans instead of the French fighting the Communists. In neighbouring Laos, four distinct armies contend for supremacy. Cambodia, another part of the former French empire in Indo-China, has been ruled with brilliant but erratic skill by Prince Sihanouk, the king turned politician; but in the spring of 1967, Cambodia too had its Communist guerrillas, and in 1968, Sihanouk talked of 'civil war'. Instability was thus the rule, not the exception.

Much of the violence and insecurity that has reigned in South-East Asia since the Second World War was probably inevitable; though demagoguery and human folly have created unrest where there need have been none. What is happening all over South-East Asia is revolution of one kind or another: either a national revolution against Western rule or even Western influence, or a social revolution inspired by the search for new standards to replace those superimposed by Western imperialism on traditional societies that are ill-adapted to meet the pressures of a dynamic and aggressive century. The most insidious, persistent, and single-minded of the revolutionaries are Communists of one kind or another. Since nearly all South-East Asia's Communists are inspired and helped from outside the area, and since the United States and other Western powers have tried to counter their progress, South-East Asia has become one of the world's major theatres of the cold war – indeed the area, above all others, where the cold war, in reality, has been 'hot'.

Sooner or later, the peoples of South-East Asia, who have ancient and distinctive histories and cultures, would have reclaimed their independence, whether by force, guile, or diplomacy. But the Second World War stimulated and canalized their national emotions. By accident rather than design, the Japanese set the spark to the powder-keg. They had come as conquerors, but they were Asians, not Europeans, and their fellow-Asians greeted them as liberators, though they soon learned to detest the arrogance and brutality of the Japanese soldiery. The coming of the Japanese, however, demonstrated two things: that the Europeans were not invincible and that the local people could rule themselves. Throughout East Asia, the concept of 'face' – a man's standing, dignity, or prestige in the eyes of his fellows – is important. The white had lost face and shed his 'burden'. Things could never be the same again. Moreover in a number of occupied countries, the Japanese set up puppet administrations which, however subservient they were to Tokyo's will, nevertheless provided a training ground for local nationalists. In this sense, too, things could never be the same again, in that it would no longer be possible for returning Europeans to argue that their Asian dependencies were incapable of governing themselves.

If local governments were a product of Japanese occupation in its 'liberating' sense, guerrilla warfare was a product of its oppressive aspect. In Burma, Malaya, Laos, and the Philippines, anti-Japanese resistance armies sprang up. In most of these resistance groups, the Communists played a leading part. In the last two years of the war, especially, there was thus an alliance of convenience between local nationalists, Communists, and the returning Westerners – British and Americans – who air-dropped or smuggled arms to them. But many of these arms were buried for future use against the Western authorities. The Burmese and Malayans and Filipinos had learnt the art of guerrilla warfare and this was particularly true of the Communists among them. In Europe, too, the partisans had learnt to shoot and some of them tried to carry the habit into peace-time. But in Europe, this phase of unrest was short-lived; in South-East Asia, it has never stopped.

To sum up: the most powerful force at work in South-East Asia since the Second World War has been nationalism; and its most energetic challenger, and occasional ally, is Communism. The involvements of the great powers have complicated an already complex situation and made it more perilous. In the first post-war phase, the retreating imperial powers – Britain, France, and Holland – were all involved in shooting wars. Since the Geneva settlement of 1954, which ended the first Indo-China war, the United States has made its presence felt. On the Communist side, the Soviet Union and China have also been involved, but only indirectly: other Communists have done this fighting.

There has long been a clear danger that the local conflicts of South-East Asia might 'escalate' into a world war. This danger is still with us, and indeed in a more acute form than ever. Through its commitment to defend Malaysia, Britain had to bear the brunt of aggression from Indonesia. But it is in Laos and Vietnam that lies the most acute danger to world peace. American-supported governments in both countries have failed to contain local Communist insurrections, master-minded from North Vietnam. The thought of defeat is, however, intolerable to the United States, which is aware that it has the power to destroy North Vietnam. The memory of Korea, on the other hand, deters the Americans from invading North Vietnam which, in turn, would probably provoke a counter-intervention from China. And should this happen, despite the Sino-Soviet dispute, the Soviet Union might find it hard to stay out of the conflict. Against this background President Johnson's response to North Vietnam's challenge has been a controlled escalation which, by 1968, has reached alarming levels.

All things considered, the dangers in South-East Asia thus look considerably more acute than those in any other area, including the Sino-Soviet border and Berlin. In more general terms, the importance of the area greatly transcends that of Africa, to which the British press has devoted disproportionate space during the past few years. That is why it is essential for English-speaking readers to have access to the facts of the South-East Asian situation in which, much against their will, they are involved. Most of them are made aware of these facts only through their newspapers or television sets which, at best, present a disjointed picture and at worst a misleading or inaccurate one. Hence this book.

In later chapters, we shall consider the crisis areas in some detail. Before that, however, we shall introduce the countries of South-East Asia, one by one or in related groups, and outline their histories, with special attention to the turbulent post-war years.

Part One PLACES AND PEOPLES

Malays must not use their left hands when eating, and Vietnamese flavour their food with a sauce called *Nuoc Mam*, made of rotting fish and sea water. A trishaw or pedicab is called a *cyclo* in Saigon and a *remorque* in Vientiane, where the driver rides in front. Indonesians wear sarongs and the delicate beauties of Vietnam float by, trailing long slit skirts, called *Ao Dai*, behind them. The Shans of Burma speak virtually the same language as the Lao of Laos. The Malays find it distasteful to eat with the Chinese because the latter eat pork, which is unclean in Islamic eyes. The Balinese practise a form of Hinduism and the Filipinos are mostly Roman Catholics.

This could go on indefinitely. The point is simply that the term 'South-East Asia' is a geographical expression and a verbal convenience, no more. The peoples of South-East Asia are more varied and more distinct from each other than those of Europe. They speak many languages and hundreds of dialects; they have different customs and religions and have often been at war with each other. Perhaps they have only two fundamental things in common: all their countries lie within the tropics, and all were ruled by despotic monarchies before the coming of the white man. Another thing could be added, for though it was transient its effects spread far and wide: the entire region was overrun by the Japanese during the Second World War. Finally, all were Western colonies – with a solitary exception: Siam.

These facts have conditioned the history of the peoples of South-East Asia and their present outlook. Tropical climates limite energies – as do tropical diseases. In other respects, however, they make life easier: tropical populations don't need wool or heavy clothing, nor do they need heating in their houses (except in the hills). Exertion is therefore less necessary than in temperate climates, and harder to furnish when needed.

The tradition of obedience and hereditary memories of despotic rule have ensured that democracy, where it has been attempted, has proved a frail plant. It has withered and died in Burma and Indonesia since independence and has little meaning in Cambodia, Laos, or South Vietnam. North Vietnam is under a totalitarian Communist dictatorship. Democracy has never really been tried in Siam. Only in Malaysia (in which the peoples were given crash courses in democracy before the British handed over) and the Philippines (where the Americans introduced democratic voting systems before anybody else) does democracy look like having any future.

As in all the underdeveloped areas of the world, the fundamental problem in South-East Asia is to bring each country to what the American economist W. W. Rostow called the stage of 'take-off', that is, self-sustaining economic growth. This was not seen to be necessary until quite recently, and the need is still not as acute in some countries as in others. Burma and Siam, Cambodia and South Vietnam (in normal times) still have plenty of land and rice surpluses for export. But if they don't reach the take-off stage within the next few years, they too will be swamped by the population explosion. Indonesia also would have plenty of land if the population were more evenly distributed. But two-thirds of its 100 million people are crowded on Java, where many were dying of starvation as these lines were written in the spring of 1964.

Primarily, take-off is a question of modernization. Old habits and lethargies have to be discarded along with superstitions. Education has to be rationalized, accelerated, and taken everywhere, and the priorities must be right: at the present stage of development, the countries of South-East Asia need graduates (especially in the sciences) far more desperately than they need toddlers in kindergartens. The modernizers in South-East Asia are few, however, and fighting an uphill battle against the entrenched forces of tradition which – with obvious exceptions – include the priesthoods. In Malaya and Indonesia, there are enlightened Moslems who want Islam to move with the times; and traditionalists, sometimes fanatical, who want to put the clock back and go so far as to rule out cooperation in any form with non-Moslems. Buddhism, too, is a problem. In a spiritual sense, it has brought consolation for this life's ills by emphasizing their transience. But in a social sense, it has the force of inertia or stagnation; moreover, it has tended – especially in Ceylon, which lies outside the scope of this book, but also in Burma and Vietnam – to play a militant part in politics.

The most powerful modernizing force in South-East Asia could be the Chinese, most of whom left the southern provinces of China in waves in the early decades of this century, and now dominate commercial life wherever they have settled – in Malaya, Siam, Indonesia, Vietnam, the Philippines, and elsewhere. Energetic and resourceful, the overseas Chinese are – or rather, ought to be – an asset to the countries that harbour them. But when the Chinese moved in, they brought their ancestral and local loyalties with them, to Kwangtung or Kwangsi, Fukien or Hainan island, together with their secret societies and an overall awareness of their Chineseness and superiority over outer barbarians. Their main interests were making money and sending back sums to their relatives at home. Their clannishness and commercial gifts made them unpopular and nearly all the countries in which they have settled have imposed disabilities of one kind or another on them. They, in turn, have shown little taste for assimilation; though assimilation is surely the only way in which their talents can be employed for the common good.

The Chinese are the latest of the migratory waves that have poured into South-East Asia; their arrival roughly coincided with the less numerically important arrival of Indians in Singapore and Malaya. In prehistoric times, the Thais and Burmese came down from China; so did the ancestors of the Vietnamese, who seem to have intermarried with local people of

Indonesian stock. South-East Asia is thus a cross-roads and a melting pot, though there has been less 'melting' – of races as well as cultures – than 'meeting'. On the South-East Asian mainland, the greatest cultural influences have been Hinduism and Theravada Buddhism from India, and Mahayana Buddhism and Confucianism from China. Buddhism supplanted Hinduism in the medieval Khmer Empire (which spread out from Cambodia) and took a deep hold in Laos, Siam, and Burma. All these countries practise the simpler Theravada Buddhism (also known as Hinayana or the Lesser Vehicle). The more complex Mahayana (Greater Vehicle) form is found chiefly in Vietnam.

To the south, Islam came to Malaya and Indonesia in the fifteenth century and supplanted Hinduism and Buddhism. In the Philippines, however, Catholicism and other Christian Churches have supplanted Islam, except in the south.

Despite the cultural and ethnic diversity of South-East Asia, it is not hard when looking at, say, the fair-skinned Laotian women or the dark-brown Cambodians to know that they both, like the middle-brown Javanese, come from South-East Asia and not from, say, Europe or Latin America or the Middle East. There is no such thing as *a* South-East Asian type; but there are recognizable South-East Asian *types*. To this extent, there is unity within diversity.

This, however, is no more than a quick glance at the area as a whole. We must now sketch the countries of South-East Asia individually.

Chapter Two ONE BY ONE

This chapter can, of course, be read in the ordinary way as just another chapter. But as the reader gets deeper into the ensuing political analysis, he may find the need to turn back to this point for reference. My aim here is simple: to give the main facts about each country as briefly as possible. It is not to argue or interpret. That comes later.

BURMA

The Union of Burma comprises Burma proper and the Shan, Kachin, Kayah, and Karen States. The total area is 262,000 square miles and the population probably exceeds twenty-two millions. There is no standard name for the inhabitants; some authorities call them 'Burmans' and others 'Burmese'. I have tried, in the main, to stick to 'Burmans' for the population as a whole and 'Burmese' for the dominant ethnic group. There are many other groups, including the Shans, Karens, Karen-nis, Pa-Os, Kachins, and Arakanese. The dominant religion is Buddhism (Theravada, Hinayana, or Lesser Vehicle), but many Arakanese are Moslems; and there are large Christian communities, mainly Baptist, among the Karens.

Burma is hilly and relatively dry in the north, flat and humid in the south. It is the largest rice exporter in the world; it is also rich in teak and other woods, oil, and various minerals.

The Burmese kings conquered their non-Burmese neighbours in the eleventh century and founded an empire that lasted 200 years and whose remains can be seen in the impressive ruins of Pagan, its capital. Burma was again unified in the sixteenth and eighteenth centuries. It was subdued by the British in 1826. Since independence, which came in 1948, Burma has been beset by insurgency. There have been two rival Communist rebellions and a number of insurrections among non-Burmese peoples resentful of control by the Burmese. U Nu's increasingly chaotic parliamentary régime was overthrown in March 1962 by a military junta headed by General Ne Win. The political philosophy of the revolutionary régime is known as Burmese Socialism. In foreign affairs it is non-aligned.

SIAM

Siam (or Thailand, its present official name) has more than $25\frac{1}{2}$ million people, living in 198,000 square miles. As in Burma, with which Siam has often been at war, Siam's religion is Buddhism of the Lesser Vehicle. There are probably $2\frac{1}{2}$ million Chinese in Siam, but many of them are assimilated and estimates vary widely. There are more Lao in north-eastern Siam than in Laos itself.

Geographically, economically, and politically, Siam is dominated by its capital, Bangkok, which has become a great international communications centre as well as the natural commercial hub of Siam itself. Siam is second only to Burma as a rice exporter. There are valuable forests in the north, tin and wolfram in the isthmus and western hills, and rubber in the south.

The Siamese city-states of Sukhothai (thirteenth and fourteenth centuries) and Ayutthaya (1350–1767) played important parts in South-East Asia in their day. The present kingdom, centred on Bangkok, was founded in 1782, and King Phumiphon Andunyadet is the ninth reigning monarch. In the nineteenth century, the Siamese escaped the West's imperial drive by playing off the British against the French. As a result, the Siam-

Places and Peoples

ese are free both of anti-colonialist complexes and of left-wing revolutionary fervour. The traditions of obedience and inequality are deeply ingrained in Siam. The habitual way of changing governments is by *coup d'état* (usually fairly bloodless). That was the way the late Marshal Sarit Thanarat came to power in 1958. When he died in December 1963, however, he was succeeded, without bloodshed, by his deputy, General Thanom Kittikachorn. In foreign affairs, Siam is aligned with the West and a member of the South-East Asia Treaty Organization (SEATO).

LAOS

Laos is a land-locked kingdom about the size of the United Kingdom (91,400 square miles) but with probably no more than two million inhabitants (the Laotians tend to double this figure for reasons that can be guessed). Only half the population are Lao; the rest are tribes of diverse origins, including the Meo, Kha, and the quaintly named White Thai and Black Thai (called after the colour of their national dress).

There are hump-backed mountains in the north and much thick jungle; the south is relatively flat. Laos is mainly at the subsistence economy level. There is a rice surplus in the south and a rice shortage in the north. Timber, green coffee, and benzoin are exported. The opium traffic, though illegal, is important. Laos is not viable without foreign aid.

The Lao, who came from Yunnan in China, founded petty States in the twelfth century. Some of these united in 1353 in the kingdom of Lan Xang (Million Elephants), whose capital was Luang Prabang. In the eighteenth century there were three rival kingdoms in Laos: at Luang Prabang, Vientiane in the centre, and Champassak in the south. Later Laos was conquered by the Siamese, whom the French drove out towards the end of the nineteenth century. Since the Geneva settlement of 1962, Laos has been theoretically united under the non-aligned government of Prince Souvanna Phouma. In fact the country is in a state of virtual civil war and, in effect, untidily partitioned into Communist and non-Communist zones.

CAMBODIA

There are more than five million Cambodians (who call themselves Khmers in memory of past glories). Present-day Cambodia covers about 70,000 square miles. Chinese and Vietnamese communities together outnumber the Khmers in Phom Penh, the capital. The religion of the Khmers is Buddhism of the Lesser Vehicle.

Only a quarter of Cambodia's arable land is under cultivation, but there is a substantial rice surplus. There are also excellent fisheries, notably in the Great Lake (Tonle Sap). Dense forest covers more than half the country.

The ruins of Angkor are among the architectural wonders of the world, the outstanding buildings being Angkor Wat (Great Temple) and the Bayon, built in the twelfth and thirteenth centuries. They are relics of the great Khmer empire, which stretched into Siam, Laos, Vietnam, and Malaya. In the earliest period, Cambodia (or Fu Nan, as it was called) became Hindu; later Buddhism took over. The French moved in in the late nineteenth century, but Cambodia regained its independence in 1954. Politically, the Head of State, Prince Sihanouk, *is* Cambodia. His *Sangkum Reastr Niyum* (Popular Socialist Community) monopolized the National Assembly until, in September1 966, he allowed relatively free elections which produced a right-wing Chamber. Since then, Cambodia has been in a state of crisis, and early in 1967 a Communist-led guerrilla campaign started. In foreign affairs, Cambodia is supposed to be non-aligned, but in practice, it leaned towards China until 1967 when relations cooled.

VIETNAM

Vietnam was the most important component of the French Indo-China empire and customs union; the other parts being Laos and Cambodia. Vietnam (North and South) covers more than 129,000 square miles and has about twenty-nine million inhabitants. Most of the people are Vietnamese but there are about 1,300,000 Chinese in Vietnam and large ethnic minorities, such as the Mois, Rhadés, and Thais. There is a hotch-potch of religions. Probably most of the people would call themselves Confucians, but there are also many Buddhists of the Greater Vehicle; adherents of various sects, such as Cao Dai (an eclectic religion) and Hoa Hao (a form of primitive Buddhism); and about two million Roman Catholics.

Economically, North and South Vietnam are complementary. The North has the coal and iron and some industries, but is short of rice; the South has a rice surplus and rubber, but its manufactures are in their infancy.

The cradle of Vietnamese (or Annamese) civilization was the Red River Delta of Tonking. Broadly speaking, Vietnamese history consists of a drive to the south and persistent attempts to resist Chinese encroachments. The Trung sisters expelled the Chinese in A.D. 40 but were later defeated. Vietnam was in fact under Chinese rule for about 1,000 years, from 111 B.C. till A.D. 939. In 1471 the southward driving Vietnamese destroyed the Champa kingdom in what is now Cochinchina. They drove on into the Mekong River Delta at the expense of the Khmer empire. Vietnam's own empire was at its greatest in the middle of the eighteenth century. The French conquest of Vietnam began in 1857 and was completed by 1883. Vietnam regained its independence in 1954 but as the outcome of that year's Geneva conference the country was partitioned into two roughly equal parts along the 17th parallel.

North Vietnam (Democratic Republic of Vietnam) is a Communist State under the presidency of Ho Chi Minh, whose provisional government was proclaimed in 1945.

South Vietnam (Republic of Vietnam) was under the authoritarian rule of President Ngo Dinh Diem from 1954 until the President was overthrown and murdered in an army *coup d'état* in November 1963. In September 1967, General Nguyen Van Thieu was elected President, with Air Marshal Nguyen Cao Ky as Vice-President; the two men had been in office as Chief of State and Premier respectively, since June 1965. Since 1958 South Vietnam has been fighting, with United States help, against a Communist insurrection directed from North Vietnam.

29

MALAYSIA, SINGAPORE, AND BRUNEI

The Federation of Malaysia was born, in the teeth of Indonesian hostility, on 16 September 1963. In its original form, it linked Malaya, Singapore, and two of the three non-Indonesian territories of Borneo: Sabah (formerly North Borneo) and Sarawak. The third, the British-protected Sultanate of Brunei, was to have joined but opted out. Relations between Malaya and Singapore deteriorated fast, largely owing to Malay extremism in Kuala Lumpur, the Federal capital, and on 9 August 1965 Singapore's Prime Minister, Mr Lee Kuan-yew, announced his territory's secession. This left Malaya – itself a federation of eleven States – Sabah, and Sarawak, making thirteen States in all.

Malaya proper is a geographical extension of Siam. Three-quarters of the peninsula's 50,700 square miles are covered in dense jungle. Malaya has displaced Indonesia as the world's largest rubber producer; it is also the world's largest producer of tin. Its seven million people include more than $2\frac{1}{2}$ million Chinese and 750,000 Indians or Pakistanis. Together with the Malays, they are called Malayans (or Malaysians if referring to the citizenship of the new Federation). With an annual income of U.S. $300 each, they compete with Formosa for the highest living standards in Asia, after Japan's.

Hinduism gave way to Islam from the fourteenth century on. The British moved into Malaya and Singapore in stages, beginning with the East India Company's occupation of Penang island in 1786, and ending in 1909 with the establishment of centralized rule. Malaya became an independent member of the Commonwealth in 1957; three years later, the Communist insurrection that had broken out in 1948 was finally defeated and the Emergency ended.

Malayan politics are dominated by Tunku Abdul Rahman's Alliance party, which groups the United Malays' National Organization (UMNO), the Malayan Chinese Association, and Malayan Indian Congress. As a result of the Malaysian federal elections in April 1964, the Alliance controls 135 of the 159 seats in the federal parliament in Kuala Lumpur. In foreign affairs, the Malaysian government is firmly anti-Communist but has stayed out of the South-East Asia Treaty Organization (SEATO). It's defence pact with Britain drew Indonesian taunts that Malaysia is a 'neo-colonialist plot'. Malayan Communist guerrillas were again active in the Thai-Malaya border area early in 1968.

Singapore has 1·7 million people, the great majority of whom are Chinese. Its area is only 225 square miles; it is the natural commercial entrepôt to the Malayan peninsula, with which it is linked by a causeway. Singapore means City of the Lion. Founded as a British colony by Sir Stamford Raffles in 1819, it was granted internal self-government in 1959. Singapore's ruling party is Mr Lee Kuan-yew's People's Action Party (PAP), which has successfully combined welfare socialism with encouragement of business. There is a Communist underground and a Communist-leaning opposition, the Socialist Front (Barisan Socialis). Singapore became a Republic, with Inche Yusuf bin Ishak as President in December 1965.

Sabah (29,400 square miles, population 455,000) was acquired by the British North Borneo Company in the 1880s. Its tribal divisions are complex, with the Dusuns the most numerous. But there are 104,000 Chinese and some 40,000 Indonesians. Rubber, timber, and copra have given Sabah prosperity, though in common with Sarawak, it is under the threat from Indonesian guerrillas. It is also the object of a territorial claim by the Philippines. Political support for Malaysia is overwhelming. The Premier is Mr Donald Stephens.

Sarawak's population of 770,000 includes 237,000 Sea Dyaks or Ibans, 229,000 Chinese, and 129,000 Malays. The area is 42,250 square miles and the mainstays of the economy are rubber, timber, and pepper. From 1841, Sarawak was an independent State ruled by the Brooke family (the White Rajahs), but it came under British protection in 1888. The last Rajah, Sir Charles Vyner Brooke, ceded the country to the British Crown in 1946. The anti-Malaysia Sarawak United People's Party – almost entirely Chinese, and Communist-infiltrated – won nearly twenty-five per cent of the vote in the 1963 elections. In addition, there is a strong Clandestine Communist

Organization which is cooperating with the Indonesian guerrillas. After a clash between Kuala Lumpur and Sarawak, the Malaysian central government's nominee, Penghulu Tawi Sli, was appointed Chief Minister on 24 September 1966.

Brunei consists of two small enclaves (2,226 square miles) within Sarawak. It has about 84,000 people, nearly all Moslems. At one time, the authority of the Sultans of Borneo extended over much of what later became British Borneo. Brunei came under British protection in 1888 and was a backwater until the late 1920s when a rich oilfield was discovered. Following a rebellion in December 1962, the Sultan suspended the constitution. He was to have brought Brunei into the Malaysian Federation but changed his mind during the 1963 negotiations, probably because of a dispute over oil revenues.

INDONESIA

The Indonesian Republic is the largest and most important country of South-East Asia. Its 3,000 islands cover 576,000 square miles of land. Some seventy per cent of its 100 million people are concentrated on Java, the smallest of its four major islands: the others are Sumatra, Celebes (Sulawesi), and Borneo (Kalimantan); the western half of New Guinea has been under Indonesian rule since May 1963. There are more than 300 ethnic groups in Indonesia and some 250 languages are spoken. The Javanese are the dominant ethnic and linguistic group, but the national language – Bahasa Indonesia (a modernized Malay) – is widely spoken. About ninety-five per cent of the people are Moslems; Bali practises a form of Hinduism; and there are scattered Christian communities totalling about five per cent of the population. There are Indian and Arab minorities and a large Chinese community (nearly three million).

Indonesia has bountiful natural resources, the most important sources of foreign exchange, in normal times, being rubber, oil, tin, and sugar. Times, however, have hardly ever been normal since independence was proclaimed in 1945. Nearly five years of fighting against the Dutch followed, and both before and since full sovereignty was achieved, on 27 December 1949, the central government has had to contend with rebellions. The most important rebels have been: the fanatical Darul Islam movement, whose followers want Indonesia to be a theocratic Islamic State, and which has been active sporadically in west Java and parts of Sumatra and Celebes; and a group of leading politicians and army officers who proclaimed a rival government of Indonesia in Sumatra in 1958 and whose followers went on fighting in Celebes until the summer of 1961. Indonesia's defence budgets were swollen during that period, most notably by the purchase of more than £130 million of Soviet arms in January 1961, mainly with the intention of dislodging the Dutch from West New Guinea. The confrontation policy against Malaysia further aggravated Indonesia's economic troubles; trade relations with Malaysia being suspended, Indonesia lost the use of Singapore as a disposal point for exports.

Hinduism and Buddhism came to the archipelago in the first three centuries A.D. The most powerful of the early kingdoms was Srividjaya, which was centred on Sumatra but controlled part of the Malay peninsula and west Java from the late seventh century. The magnificent Buddhist monument at Borobudur in Java is a legacy of the eighth-century kingdom of Kalinga. But the greatest of the Indonesian empires was the Javanese kingdom of Madjapahit in the fourteenth century. The Dutch started asserting themselves in Indonesia in the sixteenth century.

The Indonesian Republic was a parliamentary democracy, of a kind, from 1945 till 1960, though only one general election was ever held – in 1955. In 1959, President Sukarno outlined his 'concept' of a guided democracy which would do away with 'wasteful debates' and opposition parties. A Council of People's Representatives would include not only members of political parties, but representatives of 'functional groups', such as farmers, professional people, and the armed forces, on much the same pattern as Mussolini's Italy or Franco's Spain. Guided democracy would be supplemented by 'guided economy' under a National Planning Board.

On 12 March 1967, Sukarno's mandate as President was revoked and General Suharto was appointed Acting President

T – B

until general elections could be held. The decline in Sukarno's fortunes had begun in the late summer of 1965, when reports of his deteriorating health forced a showdown between the Army and the powerful Communist Party (PKI) which, at that time, had 3 million members and was the largest in the world outside the Communist countries. Six generals were murdered in a PKI-supported coup early on 1 October. Two other generals escaped: the Defence Minister, General Masution, who was wounded, and Major-General Suharto, who has since emerged as Indonesia's new strong man. The abortive coup touched off a massacre of Communists and sympathizers, in which perhaps 500,000 were killed. Suharto's government has ended the confrontation policy against Malaysia and is trying to restore Indonesia's finances.

THE PHILIPPINES

If you count all the Philippine islands, there are 7,000 of them, covering 115,600 square miles, but most of them are tiny. The Filipinos, who number nearly thirty million, speak seventy languages between them. Most of these, however, are spoken by small groups. There are eight dominant linguistic groups, including Tagalog, the official 'national' language. About ninety-two per cent of the population are at least nominally Christians, and of these eighty per cent are claimed by the Roman Catholic Church. Moslems total about four per cent, mainly in Mindanao and Sulu. The large Chinese minority numbers about 250,000, but many of these have intermarried with the predominant Malay stock and are accepted as Filipinos.

The main crops are sugar, rice, and coconuts. Timber is also important; mining includes iron and chromite ores.

Spain ruled the Philippines for 300 years. Filipino nationalism was already far advanced when the United States annexed the islands in 1899 after the Spanish–American War. The country has been independent since 1946. It has a vigorous parliamentary democracy on the American model. Strongly anti-Communist, the Philippines is a member of SEATO and sent a 2,000-man contingent to South Vietnam in September 1966. President Ferdinand E. Marcos was elected in November 1965.

Part Two NATIONALISTS AND COMMUNISTS

The present troubles of South-East Asia have deep roots going back to the turn of the century. To deal with them adequately here would, however, take up space that must be reserved for more recent events. But a few signposts can be given.

The first nationalist revolutionaries in South-East Asia were the Filipinos, who had been under Spanish rule since the sixteenth century; and the first nationalist hero was José Rizal, who was executed in Spain in 1896. About this time, precocious currents of nationalism were beginning to flow in from two major countries of East Asia: China and Japan. The Boxer uprising of 1898 gave the Chinese the emotional unity of which nations, in the modern sense, are made. The overthrow of the Manchu dynasty in 1911 and the rise of Sun Yat-sen's Kuomintang (Nationalist) party, whose first principle was 'nationalism', were powerful influences in neighbouring Annam (Vietnam) and among the scattered communities of South-East Asia. The meteoric emergence of modern Japan was another permeating influence. When Japan defeated Tsarist Russia in 1905, Asians saw for themselves that an Asian people could learn the West's technological secrets and beat the West at its own game.

In the 1920s, a new force – Communism – began for the first time to fan the flames of nationalist discontent. The first Communist International, better known as the Comintern, had been set up by Lenin in 1919, with the object of furthering Communism by propaganda or violence all over the world, under Moscow's direction. Depriving the Western countries of their colonies was part of the plan. The independence of the colonial peoples was, however, a secondary consideration. The main thing was to speed Communist revolution in the metropolitan countries, by provoking their economic collapse. Lenin and his followers believed collapse would follow the loss of the colonies. To these ends, the Comintern sent its agents to South-East Asia to set up local Communist parties.

One of these agents – and one of the most remarkable figures of contemporary South-East Asia – was Nguyen Ai Quoc of Vietnam, better known as Ho Chi Minh. Ho was active in south China, Siam, and his own Vietnam from 1925. In 1930, he created the Communist Party of Indo-China. The choice of name was significant. The term 'Indo-China' was used by the French to cover the three components of their Far Eastern empire: Vietnam (which consisted of Tonking, Annam, and Cochinchina), Laos, and Cambodia. By naming his party the Communist Party of Indo-China, Ho Chi Minh was serving notice that he intended to dislodge the French from all three territories and unite them under Vietnamese rule. The more recent history of Laos and Cambodia shows that this is by no means a fanciful theory.

Another agent of the Comintern was a dynamic, adventurous, and unscrupulous figure: the Indonesian Tan Malaka, who, by 1924, had become the Comintern's principal organizer in South-East Asia. A Communist Party of the Indies – the predecessor of the present Indonesian Communist Party (PKI) – had already been set up in 1920 by Dutch Communists. In 1925, Tan Malaka turned up in Manila, travelling as Jorge Fuentes and calling himself a musician. Engaging and persuasive, he soon made his mark with the Filipino nationalists; but the Americans had him deported in 1927. The following year, however, a Communist-led Workers' Party was set up in the Philippines; and in 1930, it was transformed into the Communist Party of the Philippines. Tan Malaka was also active in Malaya and Singapore, but it was Chinese agents who, in 1928, set up the South Seas Communist Party in Singapore – the forerunner of the Malayan Communist Party (1930).

In later 'incarnations', Tan Malaka became, in turn, a Japanese agent and a kind of free-lance Communist, before being executed by the Indonesian army in 1949. His legend lives on, and no book on contemporary South-East Asia can ignore him. But in today's perspective, Tan Malaka seems much less important than Ho Chi Minh, whose story is fundamental to an understanding of Indo-China, the major crisis area in the whole region.

In the early years that now concern us, the Communists were too confident. In Indonesia, Singapore, and the Philippines, they tried to set up Soviet States. These attempts all came to grief, and the Communist leaders were gaoled. In 1930, a French Communist was arrested in Singapore and gave away all the Comintern's secrets in China and South-East Asia. As a result, most of the Malayan Communists were arrested, and in Hong Kong in 1931, Ho Chi Minh (still calling himself Nguyen Ai Quoc) was gaoled by the British. Broadly speaking, the Communist movement throughout South-East Asia was now out of harm's way until the Second World War.

Chapter Two

COLLABORATORS AND RESISTERS
IN THE SECOND WORLD WAR

Between December 1941 and mid-1942, the Japanese occupied
Malaya and Singapore, Burma, the Dutch East Indies, and the
Philippines. Their rule also reached indirectly to French Indo-
China and Siam. In 1940, when France fell, the Gaullist
authorities in Indo-China had been replaced by Petainists;
and in September, the new men signed a treaty entrusting the
defence of Indo-China to Japan. The Siamese, collaborating
with Japan, saw in this a good opportunity of regaining the
Cambodian and Laotian territory which they had ceded to the
French half a century earlier. In May 1941, under a treaty signed
in Tokyo, the French signed away their rights over Laotian
territories on the right bank of the Mekong, and two Cambodian
provinces. These the Siamese took over. Later, the Japanese
handed the Siamese (who had signed an alliance with them) the
northern Malay States, seized from the Siamese kings by the
British in the nineteenth century. These successive recoveries of
lost territory, though they gratified Siam's pride in its own imperial past, did nothing to endear the Siamese to their Laotian,
Cambodian, and Malay neighbours. At the end of the war,
however, Siam had to return the seized territories and was back
where it started.

Though Japan's new order did not last long, the Japanese
occupation of South-East Asia was a turning point. The Western

powers had been defeated and humiliated; and the victors were Asians. Moreover, the Japanese gave the peoples of the occupied countries a chance to show they could administer their own affairs.

South-East Asia's war-time experience should be looked at through Asian eyes. The insult implicit in the Western term 'collaborator' had relatively little relevance in Asian minds. In France or Holland, the collaborators were citizens of free countries under enemy occupation. But in Burma or the Philippines, the people were under colonial rule; the Japanese had come as enemies of their own enemies, and many local nationalists saw the invaders as liberators. Hence while some patriots took to the hills it was natural for others to work with the Japanese. Equally understandably, there was sometimes collusion between collaborators and resisters, as a form of reinsurance for those who did not come out on the winning side.

As the Japanese occupation wore on, however, many of the 'collaborators', resenting the conquerors' arrogance and brutality, joined the resisters. In this second phase, the Communists found the chance they had been waiting for to identify themselves with the nationalists. In Malaya and the Philippines, the Communists achieved the leadership of the resistance groups; in Burma and Indonesia, on the other hand, the leadership remained in nationalist hands, even though the Communists played a part in the resistance. The seeds of today's turmoil were sown in this second war-time phase.

Let us now look at collaboration and resistance in individual countries.

THE PHILIPPINES

When Japan invaded the Philippines, President Quezón and Vice-President Osmeña set up an exile government in the United States. Most of the nationalists who stayed behind collaborated. One of them, José Laurel, formerly a justice of the Supreme Court, became the President of an 'independent' Philippine Republic proclaimed under Japanese auspices in September 1943.

Long before this – in March 1942 – the Communist Party had set up a resistance movement with a nationalist-sounding name: the People's Anti-Japanese Resistance Army, usually known as the Hukbalahap from its initial syllables in Tagalog (*Hukbong Bayan Laban Sa Hapon*), or Huk for short. The Huk training school, in Central Luzon, was under Chinese instructors from Mao Tse-tung's Eighth Route Army. The Huk leader, Luis Taruc, found his recruits among the illiterate and destitute peasantry, who knew nothing about Marxism but plenty about the moneylenders and absentee landlords who exploited them. The Huks emerged from hiding – between October 1944, when the returning Americans landed at Leyte, and February 1945, when General MacArthur captured Manila – and set about establishing a 'People's democratic government'. MacArthur, however, disbanded their organization and had Taruc arrested, though he was not held for long.

BURMA

In Burma, the nationalists greeted the Japanese unreservedly as liberators. Calling themselves Thakins ('masters') to show they were equal to their British rulers, the nationalists were dominated by a spell-binding personality, Aung San, who later headed Burma's pre-independence government. In 1940, the Japanese had smuggled Aung San and twenty-nine other Thakins, including Ne Win, Burma's military dictator of the 1960s, to Japan. There, the 'Thirty Comrades' were trained to be the officers of a projected anti-British Burma Independence Army. By the time the Japanese invaded Burma, Aung San and his guerrillas were in position, ready to help the advancing Japanese. In August 1943, Japan proclaimed Burma's 'independence' and set up a puppet government under Dr Ba Maw. But the fascist character of Ba Maw's régime, together with the excesses of the Japanese, turned Aung San and his friends against the occupiers.

By 1944, the bulk of the Thakins had rallied around Aung San who was organizing the anti-Japanese resistance. The dividing line between Communists and nationalists was blurred, for all the revolutionaries called themselves Marxists. Aung San himself, though probably not a true Communist, worked closely with the Communists. He had built up a People's Freedom League, with his Japanese-trained Independence Army at its core; and the Communist leader, Thakin Soe, had formed an Anti-Fascist Organization. In 1944, these two organizations merged to form the Anti-Fascist People's Freedom League (AFPFL), which became Burma's ruling party after independence. But Aung San and Thakin Soe soon fell out, and we shall meet Soe again in later chapters.

The rest of Aung San's career can be summarized in little space. In May 1945, he went to Ceylon to meet Admiral Lord Mountbatten, the Allied Supreme Commander in South-East Asia. As a result, Aung San's guerrillas later helped the British mop up the retreating Japanese. In London, eighteen months later, Aung San negotiated with Clement Attlee the agreement that led to Burma's independence. But when independence came on 4 January 1948, Aung San was not there to enjoy it: he was murdered, together with most of his pre-independence cabinet, on 19 July 1947. It was thus that U Nu, who had until then played a far less militant role in Burman politics than Aung San, became independent Burma's first Prime Minister.

INDONESIA AND MALAYA

In the East Indies and Malaya, the Japanese moved more cautiously in setting up 'independent' States.

Along with other Indonesian nationalists, Sukarno had been released from Dutch internment by the Japanese military. He became one of the collaborators, as chairman of an Indonesian Central Advisory Council set up by the Japanese. Another leading nationalist, Sutan Sjahrir, went into hiding and set up resistance groups. Sjahrir's resistance network was the most active and successful, but it was not the only one. There was also a less active Communist-led group, under Sjarifuddin. The Japanese, however, showed themselves adaptable, as well as cautious, in Indonesia. In 1944, after they had promised Indonesia its independence, they started schools 'for the study of nationalism *and Marxism*'. One of the lecturers was Sjahrir; another was our old acquaintance, Tan Malaka, who had broken with the Comintern and taken refuge in Japan.

The Marxist experiment was, however, short-lived. In March 1945, with defeat looming, the Japanese created an Independence Preparatory Committee, headed – as the Central Advisory Council had been – by Sukarno. On 8 August, Sukarno was summoned to Japanese-occupied Saigon and told independence was imminent. Nine days later – that is, two days after Japan's surrender – Sukarno proclaimed the Indonesian Republic, with himself as President and Mohammed Hatta as Vice-President.

In Malaya, the nationalism with which the Communists, as elsewhere, sought to identify themselves, was not, in any valid sense, a Malayan sentiment. The Japanese flattered the Malays and persecuted the Chinese. The Malayan Communist Party (MCP) was overwhelmingly Chinese in membership and in effect was a prolongation of the Chinese Communist Party. It was thus a Chinese, not a Malayan, nationalism that the MCP identified itself with.

The MCP nevertheless had the pretension of acting on behalf of *all* Malaya's communities. Hence the names of the two organizations it set up: the Malayan People's Anti-Japanese Army (MPAJA) and the Malayan People's Anti-Japanese Union (MPAJU). The 'army' had two purposes: to terrorize the population by executions of 'traitors', and to fight the Japanese – in that order. The 'union' extended Communist authority over the villages and organized the procurement of food, and intelligence.

In 1943, Force 136 – an organization set up under Admiral Lord Mountbatten's South-East Asia Command to help resistance movements – made contact with the MPAJA. Most of the arms supplied by Force 136 remained in Communist hands after the war. Between 15 August 1945, when the Japanese collapsed, and 5 September, when Mountbatten's forces reached Singapore, the MCP, emerging from the jungle, had set up what proved to be a short-lived reign of terror. The leader of the MPAJA, Ch'in P'eng, was nevertheless invited to London for the Victory parade and awarded the O.B.E.

It was only in the summer of 1945, when the end of their militarist adventure was in sight, that the Japanese convened a meeting of Malays in Kuala Lumpur to work for Malaya's independence. Speakers described a tentative Japanese project to create a Greater Indonesia, including the Malay peninsula. It is ironical, in the light of the present hostility between Indonesia and the Federation of Malaysia, to recall that Dr Sukarno was one of these speakers.

Chapter Three
INDO-CHINA 1945–54: A SPECIAL CASE

THE GROWTH OF THE VIET MINH

In the countries we have been looking at, the Communists, broadly speaking, were the hangers-on of nationalist or peasant movements. In Indo-China, however, at least at the outset, Communism and nationalism merged into one stream of resistance to French colonialism. This important difference reflects the charismatic appeal of Ho Chi Minh as a patriotic leader.

Released from his Hong Kong gaol in 1933, Ho turned up in south China in 1941. In May, with the approval of the Chinese Nationalist provincial authorities, he called a congress of Vietnamese nationalists, from which emerged the famous Viet Minh. The full name of this body, which later became synonymous with 'Communist', was *Vietnam Doc Lap Dong Minh Hoi*, or League for the Independence of Vietnam.

A younger man than Ho, fanatically anti-French and with a special bent for guerrilla war, was sent to Vietnam by the Viet Minh to set up a clandestine organization. His name was Vo Nguyen Giap. By the time the Japanese were defeated, he had 10,000 men under arms. At some stage, probably in 1942, Giap seems to have been to Yenan with the Chinese Communists. He returned a formidable exponent of Mao Tse-tung's theories of revolutionary war.

Three Far Eastern and three Western peoples were involved

46

in Vietnam in 1945. On the Asian side: the Japanese, the Chinese (Nationalists), and the Vietnamese themselves; on the Western side: the French, British, and Americans.

The Japanese, on the run everywhere and harassed by the Viet Minh guerrillas, decided to take over in Indo-China from the Vichy authorities who, by this time, had lost their mandate. Within twenty-four hours of an ultimatum presented on 9 March 1945, the Japanese overwhelmed all French garrisons in Indo-China.

On the Vietnamese side, another important figure now comes on to the stage: the Emperor of Annam, Bao Dai. History will not record only the bad side of Bao Dai, 'the Emperor of the Casinos', who lazed away on the French Riviera during the agonizing days of Dien Bien Phu. In the 1930s, reigning under French authority, he had tried to bring in reforms but had been frustrated by the colonial administration. His Minister of the Interior, then obscure, was Ngo Dinh Diem, who soon resigned rather than put up with French interference.

Now, in March 1945, the Japanese decided to use Bao Dai. On 9 March, they arrested him, told him to proclaim the independence of Vietnam and form a government. With little choice, Bao Dai complied; but events showed he intended Vietnam's independence to become a reality.

Neither the Communists nor the nationalists recognized Bao Dai's puppet government. Diem refused to serve on it. As for Ho, he had already set up a provisional government. On 6 August, the United States Air Force dropped an atom bomb on Hiroshima; and the day after, Ho Chi Minh set up a Vietnamese People's Liberation Committee under his own chairmanship. On 18 August, Bao Dai addressed an appeal to General de Gaulle, couched in language the nobility of which ought to have appealed to the General. He wrote, for instance:

You have suffered too much during four deadly years not to understand that the Vietnamese people, who have a history of twenty centuries and an often glorious past, no longer wish, can no longer support, any foreign domination.

De Gaulle, however, knew little of Indo-China and had

other things on his mind. His first priority in external affairs was to restore France's authority over every part of its overseas empire. He ignored Bao Dai's appeal.

Ho and his followers well understood the potential value of Bao Dai as Emperor, and custodian – in his people's eyes – of the Mandate of Heaven. They set out to win the Mandate for themselves, by persuading Bao Dai to abdicate, hand over the Imperial Seals, and join them. Again Bao Dai complied, and went to Hanoi late in August to become Ho Chi Minh's Supreme Adviser. On 28 August, Ho dissolved the Liberation Committee and set up a second provisional government with the key posts in Communist hands. And on 2 September, he proclaimed the independence of Vietnam in a document that invoked the American Declaration of Independence and France's Declaration of the Rights of Man – but made no mention of the Communist Manifesto. This was supposed to be a nationalist occasion.

Now the Chinese – the third of the Asian peoples involved in these events – started moving in to occupy Indo-China north of the 16th parallel, as laid down by the Potsdam conference, from which France was absent. Thus in the crucial days of the provisional government and the proclamation of independence, the Viet Minh were dealing, not with the French colonial authorities, but with those earlier colonizers, the Chinese. This suited Ho well.

The French, meantime, were going through humiliating days. A dashing young Resistance leader, Jean Sainteny, had been sent to Kunming, in China, where he headed M5, a French intelligence network, and set about regrouping scattered French forces in the Tonking border region. Sainteny was determined to re-establish the French presence in Tonking, but was up against opposition from the Vietnamese, Chinese, and Americans. A fascinating little sideline war of the intelligence services began between M5 and the American OSS (Office of Strategic Services). The United States was determined not to allow the French to reassert their authority, and the OSS developed close relations with the Viet Minh.

Sainteny nevertheless persuaded the Americans to fly him

and four companions to Hanoi in a Dakota; but with them went the regional chief of the o s s, Patti. Sainteny and his friends took possession of the French Governor-General's palace and Giap himself led a Viet Minh delegation to make contact with him. The timing was superb. He met Giap on 27 August and next day Ho announced his second provisional government. Patti, however, persuaded the Viet Minh to stand firm against French propositions, assuring them of full American support. In later years, the Americans came to regret this support for the Vietnamese Communists, but in fairness to them, the Viet Minh's nationalist label looked pretty convincing at the time. Much of the subsequent French bitterness against American policy in South-East Asia can, however, be traced back to the war of the intelligence services in 1945.

Under the Potsdam agreements, the British were to occupy southern Indo-China. Major-General Douglas Gracey's mixed British–Indian force landed in Saigon from the first week of September. Unlike the Chinese and the Americans, the British had no wish to keep the French out, but General Leclerc's force did not start arriving until 3 October. They found a situation of unutterable confusion. The Viet Minh had set up a provisional executive before Gracey's arrival. Gracey freed the French prisoners-of-war and armed them, and the Viet Minh reacted by massacring French civilians and setting up a network of guerrilla bands. On all sides, politico-religious Resistance groups, or plain bandits, were emerging to take over this territory or that. The French set about reconquering Vietnam from the south northward.

Although the French were unaware of it, they were entering into a collision course with destiny. The idea of giving independence to dependent peoples was still remote from French official minds. This indeed was implicit in the centralist concept of France's *mission civilisatrice*. Autonomy or freedom of speech, or equality of rights with French citizens, or even French citizenship itself: all these were conceivable. But not independence. Indeed General de Gaulle's provisional government, in a declaration on 24 March 1945, offered the Indo-Chinese peoples 'freedom' and 'economic autonomy' *within a French union*: but no more.

Given this attitude, any French negotiations, whether with Communists or nationalists, were bound either to fail or to yield agreements to be broken by either side. This is just what happened in two important sets of negotiations between the French Fourth Republic and the Vietnamese. In the first set, the French were dealing with Ho Chi Minh, first in Hanoi, then in Dalat and finally in France, at Fontainebleau. They ended in failure in September 1946. Two months later, on 19 December 1946, Giap launched a general offensive against the French forces in Tonking. It was the beginning of the first Indo-China war.

In the second series of negotiations, the Vietnamese negotiator was Bao Dai. Though he had served under Ho Chi Minh as Supreme Adviser, he soon became aware of the Communist character of the provisional government and broke with it, taking refuge in Hong Kong. The French waited a year after the outbreak of war before turning to him in December 1947.

The French had turned to Bao Dai because they hoped he would prove a rallying point for nationalists who, like him, were disillusioned with the Communists. It was argued that in this way Vietnamese nationalist support would be drained away from the Viet Minh who, once isolated, could be defeated militarily. It was not, in itself, a bad idea, but its execution was vitiated from the first by the fundamental French unwillingness to concede the substance of independence.

In the earlier negotiations, Ho had insisted on two principles: *independence* and *unity*, meaning the unification of the three provinces of Vietnam: Tonking, Annam, and Cochinchina. The French, however, made a distinction between Tonking and Annam, which were protectorates, on the one hand, and Cochinchina, which was a colony, on the other. They were willing to loosen their hold slightly on the protectorates but not at all on the colony. And of course they were not willing to give full independence to any of them. When they turned to Bao Dai, they expected him to be pliant where Ho had been tough, but they were soon disappointed. Like Ho, Bao Dai insisted on unity as well as independence. In the end, he was given unity and what the French defined as 'independence in the framework of the French Union' (*au sein de l'Union Française*). This was less than he had hoped for, but he signed the agreements of March 1949 and returned to Vietnam on 28 April. He soon found how far his country's new status fell short of full independence; and the French, on their side, discovered that the 'Bao Dai solution' had solved nothing.

CAMBODIA AND LAOS

Though Vietnam is by far the most important country in the Indo-China peninsula a few words must be spared for its two neighbours, Cambodia and Laos.

The Japanese *coup* of 9 March 1945 against the Vichy authorities took place in Cambodia and Laos as well as Vietnam. On that day a Japanese plane landed on Cambodian soil carrying one of those picturesque and slightly irrational nationalist-adventurers who are so numerous in South-East Asia's history, Son Ngoc Thanh. This is a Vietnamese name and, like many other prominent Cambodians, Thanh had Vietnamese blood in his veins. A former teacher of Pali – the 'Latin' of Cambodia – Thanh had placed himself under Japanese protection in 1942, and the Japanese had groomed him for puppet stardom. Now, in March 1945, they made him Foreign Minister, and five months later, on 10 August, on the eve of Japan's defeat, he became Prime Minister. His hour of glory, however, was short-lived. On 15 September* a party of British and French officers abducted him and brought him to Saigon. He was later sentenced to twenty years' forced labour for 'threatening the external security of the State'.

With Thanh out of the way, the French negotiated a *modus vivendi* agreement with more accommodating Cambodians. Though this agreement, signed on 7 January 1946, was limited

* Donald Lancaster says (on page 134 of *The Emancipation of French Indo-China*, O.U.P., 1961) that this incident took place in October. I was given the date of 15 September by French official sources in Cambodia in 1952.

in scope, it did bring Cambodians for the first time into certain administrative posts and was a stage on the path towards autonomy. Finally, on 8 November 1949, France recognized Cambodia's 'independence within the framework of the French Union' under a treaty similar to the earlier one with Vietnam.

However, the last had not been heard of Son Ngoc Thanh, whom the French had treated with almost quixotic leniency. Despite his long gaol sentence, they placed him under house arrest in Nice, then set him free and repatriated him in November 1951. Thanh promptly started touring the country making anti-French speeches. On 9 March 1952 – symbolically, the anniversary of his return to Cambodia in a Japanese plane – he went into the jungle to join the 'Free Khmer' (*Khmer Issarak*) guerrilla groups set up by his followers after his abduction in 1945. The Khmer Issarak joined forces with the Viet Minh bands then harassing the French, and at the Geneva conference in 1954 the Communists made a strong attempt to have the Issarak and Viet Minh guerrillas recognized as legitimate Cambodian authorities. Much play was made with Son Ngoc Thanh's name as an alleged national hero and with another name, which, as far as I am aware, did not belong to anybody, living or dead: 'Son Ngoc Minh', who was said to be the leader of the Viet Minh guerrillas. The official Cambodian delegation strenuously and successfully resisted these pressures and pretensions – rightly so, for Thanh's bands numbered only three or four thousand men and the Viet Minh's groups under 'Son Ngoc Minh' only a few hundreds. In the event, the Hanoi-directed Viet Minh regulars who had been fighting the French in Cambodia were evacuated and Cambodia emerged from the Geneva conference with its national territory intact. This is an important fact, for it enabled Prince Sihanouk, the Cambodian Chief of State, to lead his country, with brilliant if erratic skill, along a neutralist path that was barred to his divided neighbours in Vietnam and Laos. As for Son Ngoc Thanh, he eventually took refuge in Siam and continued to drive Prince Sihanouk into periodic bouts of rage with his plotting.

In Laos, as elsewhere, the Japanese occupation and defeat

brought its nationalist complications. To understand these, and much of what followed when Laos was in the news between 1959 and 1962, one must remember Laotian dynastic rivalries. Prince Souvanna Phouma, the neutralist Prime Minister of Laos, and his half-brother Prince Souphannouvong, the Communist leader, belong to the junior branch of the Laotian royal family and have never been on good terms with the present king, Savang Vatthana, or his late father, Sisavang Vong. Another prince, Boun Oum, also much in the news between 1959 and 1962, comes from Champassak in the south, which was once a separate kingdom. These rivalries, which played an important part behind the scenes in the later Laotian crises, came to the fore in 1945. On 9 March, when the Japanese overthrew the French authorities, French troops and civilians, who had developed Gaullist tendencies, set up an anti-Japanese resistance movement in the south. Prince Boun Oum joined them and helped them in various ways.

Four years earlier, in an effort to counter the seduction of Siamese pan-Thai propaganda, the French had encouraged the Laotians to set up a 'young Lao' movement. In 1945 this was transformed into the Free Lao (*Lao Issara*) with independence as its main platform. The Chinese Nationalists, moving into Laos after Japan's defeat, encouraged the Lao Issara, whose leader, Prince Pethsarat, elder brother of Souvanna and Souphannouvong,* proclaimed the independence of Laos on 1 September and some weeks later deposed King Sisavang Vong. In the spring, however, the French, with Boun Oum's help, fought their way back northward. The king was restored, with Boun Oum as his Prime Minister. The Lao Issara government took refuge in Siam, where it soon split, with Souphannouvong openly joining the Viet Minh. On 27 August, the French and Laotian governments signed a *modus vivendi* agreement, similar to the earlier one with Cambodia; and four years later, on 19 July 1949, France duly recognized the independence of Laos with the usual formula of a formal place in the French Union.

* Laotian royalty allow themselves many wives and concubines. Hence a prevalence of princely half-brothers.

South-East Asia in Turmoil

We have seen how the failure of the French negotiations with Ho Chi Minh was followed soon after by the Viet Minh attack of 19 December 1946. Seven and a half years later – weary, horrible, dispiriting years – the Viet Minh army, by now grown powerful in firing power as well as in spirit, closed in on the French Union garrison defending the fortress of Dien Bien Phu in Tonking near the Laotian border. The final attack was launched on the night of 6 May 1954, and the outcome was one of the major Communist triumphs in Asia and a crushing defeat for the West in general as well as for France in particular. By any standards this was an astounding feat for that ragged band of rubber-soled coolies, the Viet Minh army, to pull off. How had they done it?

This is an important question, with an obvious but neglected bearing on the plight the Americans have found themselves in ten years later, in the second Indo-China war, against the same adversary. There are three short answers to it: the military genius of Vo Nguyen Giap, the logistic help of China after the Communist victory there in 1949, and the Communist mastery of a kind of war the French didn't even begin to understand until after their defeat: *revolutionary* war.

We have already seen how Giap built up a guerrilla force of 10,000 men in Tonking in the closing stages of the Second World War. By the end of 1946, when he launched his first assault on the French positions, he had trained six times that number, but had only two rifles to every three men. His initial failure to oust the French made him realize that this was bound to be a protracted war, and he laid his plans accordingly. The French had pursued the Viet Minh army northward into the hills along the China border and there Giap regrouped his men, retrained them and settled down to some hard thinking.

Nothing of great military consequence happened after that for nearly three years. Then in November 1949, there was a fateful development: Mao Tse-tung's armies reached the Tonking border. Now Giap's men had a sanctuary and the assurance of logistic help. On the French side there had been a false sense of security. The main military effort was being made in Cochin-china in the south, where Viet Minh terrorists were gradually extending their hold over the villages. In the north, Giap seemed to have been defeated, and the Maginot-minded French command sheltered behind the string of French-held forts along the China border: Lao Kay, Ha Giang, Cao Bang, Lang Son, and Mon Cay. When the news came that the Chinese Communists had reached the border, they did divert troops from north to south; but they seemed to have been quite unprepared for the blow Giap was preparing.

Giap did not, in fact, strike until 1 October 1950, almost a year after the arrival of the Chinese forces. His men had infiltrated into the 100-mile-wide strip of jungle to the south, separating the French fortress garrisons from the bulk of the French army. One by one the forts were overrun. By 17 October, it was all over: all the border forts were in Viet Minh hands. It was France's first major defeat of the Indo-China war. The French had lost 6,000 men and arms enough for a whole division.

Though this was a victory indeed from the Viet Minh's viewpoint, Giap seems to have decided in retrospect that he had made a strategic error. The suddenness and completeness of his own victory seems to have taken him by surprise, and he wasn't ready for the follow-through. We know, both from documents captured by the French and from Giap's published works, that there was a good deal of heated discussion within the Viet Minh high command at that time. In the end, in the light of the ease with which the French had been dislodged from their strong-points and reports of sagging morale in France, Giap decided that the time had come to throw the French into the sea. By then, in January 1951, Giap had eighty-one battalions under arms. On 13 January, he began his drive towards Hanoi.

The Viet Minh, however, were now up against a different opponent. A dashing and dynamic figure, General (later Marshal) de Lattre de Tassigny, had arrived in Vietnam in mid-December to take over supreme command throughout French Indo-China. '*Le roi Jean*', they soon called him, and, indeed, de Lattre was a king and a prima donna as well as a first-class tactician. His effect on local morale was dramatic and immediate.

55

He took personal charge of operations and on 14 January the two armies clashed at Vinh Yen, only thirty miles north-west of Hanoi. It was a bloody and merciless battle, the French countering the Viet Minh's human wave tactics with high explosive and napalm. This time the French came out on top and the Viet Minh lost 6,000 killed and 500 captured.

There was one other major battle in this phase of the war: the protracted struggle, lasting four months, for Hoa Binh, a strongpoint thirty miles south-west of Hanoi. De Lattre rightly reckoned that by taking Hoa Binh, he would cut the Viet Minh's north–south supply line. He captured it easily enough, in November 1951, but soon found his men locked in a continuous fight with the surrounding Viet Minh attackers. Then de Lattre fell seriously ill and was flown back to France, where he died in January 1952. A month later, the French decided they had had enough and pulled out of Hoa Binh without further losses. Shortly afterwards I arrived in Hanoi, where I had a long talk with the French commander in Tonking, General de Linarès. Two remarks he made seem significant. One was: 'What I like most about the withdrawal from Hoa Binh is that it was a manoeuvre of perfect military orthodoxy.' The other was a tribute to Giap: 'I wish I had him on my side.'

THE DÉBÂCLE

The battles of the border forts, and of Vinh Yen and Hoa Binh, had shown two things: that the Viet Minh army was not yet strong enough to defeat the French, and that the French, for their part, would need far more men than they were likely to get from France, 8,000 miles away, if they were ever to annihilate the Viet Minh forces and recapture the whole of Tonking. A simpler way of saying the same thing is that a prolonged stalemate, though never an inactive one, was on the way. On the French side the aggressive heart had dropped out of the struggle with de Lattre's death. His successor, notorious in later years for the part he was to play in Algerian events, was the colourless, defeatist General Salan. Up north, however, an able and energetic group of French officers were doing their best to draw the

Viet Minh forces out and force them to give battle, in the hope of inflicting heavy losses on them as at Vinh Yen. But no enemy could be more elusive. Time and again, the French tried to close a circle on groups of Viet Minh troops, regular or irregular; but the circle would close, meeting in the centre without a trace of the enemy.

And so on . . . until Navarre and Dien Bien Phu. That this was one of the decisive battles of contemporary history is beyond dispute, but controversy still rages in France over General Henri Navarre and his ill-fated choice of a place for a final military showdown with Giap's forces. The choice of Navarre himself as Supreme Commander was odd. A military intelligence officer, colourless and diffident of personality, 'his connexion with Indo-China was alleged to have been limited to arranging for the discreet surveillance of Ho Chi Minh's contacts and activities during the Fontainebleau conference'.* Arriving in Indo-China in May 1953, Navarre was appalled to find that the Viet Minh, despite the presence of more than 100,000 French Union troops, controlled 5,000 of the 7,000 villages in Tonking's ricebowl, the Red River Delta. He knew he couldn't hope to score a complete victory over the Viet Minh army, but he planned to increase the forces under his command in numbers and firing power (with American help) and fight the enemy to a standstill and a negotiated truce on the Korean model. This was what the so-called 'Navarre plan' amounted to.

But there was a complication. In April, just before Navarre's appointment, the Viet Minh regular army had invaded Laos and come almost within shouting distance of Luang Prabang, the royal capital (as distinct from Vientiane, the administrative one). On withdrawing, the Viet Minh had left behind in the two northern provinces the 'Red Prince', Souphannouvong, and a rudimentary administration calling itself the Pathet Lao ('Lao State') which claimed to be the only legitimate government of Laos. There was no telling when the Viet Minh would return, and in Paris it had been decided that Laos must be defended at all costs.

This fact, more than any other, seems to have weighed in

* *The Emancipation of French Indo-China*, by Donald Lancaster.

57

Navarre's mind in picking Dien Bien Phu, which was only a few miles from the Laotian border on the Tonking side, as the place to draw enemy fire. In all other respects, however, it was a crazy choice: Dien Bien Phu was 200 miles from Hanoi and had to be supplied by air; it was in a basin, surrounded by hills and wide open to artillery fire. This last point didn't seem to worry Navarre, whose information was that the Viet Minh lacked heavy guns in the area, and the means to bring them in. Moreover, Navarre's intelligence had estimated that the Viet Minh would be unable to maintain more than *two* divisions and *20,000* coolies in the area. This estimate was catastrophically wrong. In fact, for months on end, *80,000* coolies, wheeling bicycles laden with arms and food through the jungle, were able to keep *four* Viet Minh divisions supplied.

Dien Bien Phu had been occupied by the French on 20 November 1953. In December the Viet Minh struck again in Laos, as the French had thought they would. But it was only a diversion. Giap had seen the chance Navarre was giving him at Dien Bien Phu, and was building up his forces in the surrounding hills. By January 1954 the build-up looked threatening and Navarre was losing his initial confidence. In March the Viet Minh began to attack in earnest and the world's headlines reflected the agony and heroism of the beleaguered garrison, whose composition was typical of the French Union army: one-third Vietnamese, one-quarter Foreign Legion men, twenty-two per cent metropolitan Frenchmen and the remaining one-fifth Africans, mainly from Morocco. Despite Navarre's information, heavy guns *had* reached the Viet Minh from China and were being used to deadly effect. On the night of 6 May 1954 the last human wave overwhelmed the defenders. It was the end of the Indo-China war and indeed the beginning of the end of the French presence in Indo-China. In Asian terms it was more than a victory and more than a Communist victory: it was a demonstration, recalling Japan's defeat of Russia half a century earlier, that Asians could defeat Europeans in battle.

THE INVISIBLE WAR

But so far I have described only the top of the iceberg: the visible war. The invisible part was by far the more important. Without it Giap could never have launched his successful final offensive; without it indeed the French might have fought on even after Dien Bien Phu. That is what Navarre had said they would do, but it was hopeless, for the Red River Delta, as the French themselves said, was rotten – *pourri*. The invisible war had seen to that.

To understand what Indo-China's invisible war was about, one has to turn to the theoretical text-books as well as to the accounts of the men who lived through it. Three names are important, one of them world-famous, the second pretty well known by now and the third unknown outside a small circle of specialists: Mao Tse-tung, Vo Nguyen Giap, and Truong Chinh. Mao, chairman of the Chinese Communist Party, poet, and uncrowned emperor of China, hardly needs an introduction. Giap we have already met more than once in these pages. Though less well known, Truong Chinh is about as important as Giap in Ho Chi Minh's Democratic Republic of Vietnam. His real name is Dang Xuan Khu, and Truong Chinh, his adopted name, means 'long march' – a useful identification tag, for Truong Chinh, unlike most of his colleagues in a historically anti-Chinese country, advocates whole-hearted collaboration between North Vietnam and China. Truong Chinh is regarded as a leading Party theorist, mainly on the basis of two short works: *The August Revolution*, written in 1945 and 1946, and *The Resistance Will Win*, written in 1947. Both constitute guides to action for Vietnamese Communists in difficult circumstances. The second is the more important for the needs of this chapter.

There is one fundamental thing in common in the writings of Mao, Giap, and Truong Chinh: the emphasis given to politics as the handmaiden of tactics in the strategy of revolutionary war. This is the secret of the Communist military successes in China and Vietnam. By neglecting this hidden heart of Giap's strategy, the French hastened their own defeat; and by concentrating on the gimmickry of 'counter-insurgency', from helicopters to chemical defoliants, while overlooking the need for political action, the South Vietnamese government and its American advisers played into the hands of the Viet Cong guerrillas in the second Indo-China war.

Revolutionary war is in fact a struggle for the minds and bodies of the people among whom the irregulars live and fight. If the people are with the guerrillas, concealment and food supplies become easy; so does intelligence about the enemy's movements. It is not by coincidence that in the two Indo-China wars the unsuccessful army has been the one associated with white foreigners, French and American, who seemed to conform to the Communist description of them as 'foreign imperialists'. On the Communist side, in contrast, there have been no Russians or even Chinese in actual combat; whatever their politics, the Viet Minh of the first Indo-China war and the Viet Cong of the second were undeniably Vietnamese. Unlike the French or Americans, they were able to merge with the surrounding population, thus conforming to Mao Tse-tung's famous dictum comparing the relationship between the army and the people to that between the fish and water. True, in the first Indo-China war, many of the combatants on the French side were Vietnamese, while in the second the Americans played only a minor part as combatants (and indeed maintained the fiction that they were there only as 'advisers'). But in both wars, the Vietnamese regulars were visibly associated with foreign armies and pursuing a policy of repression, or at any rate suppression.

It would be a mistake, however, to suppose that the Communist guerrillas were universally or spontaneously accepted as liberators by the peasants among whom they moved. In both Indo-China wars, terrorism played an important part in Communist tactics. The technique was to murder village headmen or other notables and exhibit their bodies in public with a note pinned to their clothing describing the victims as 'traitors'. After a few murders in each village, the lesson went home and the authorities ran out of candidates for the jobs. Execution or torture was likewise reserved for villagers who betrayed the Communists or failed to provide them with food and shelter without question. By blows or torture, men were recruited into the guerrilla forces; once they had taken part in an operation, they were outlaws, wanted men, who tended to stay with the guerrillas for fear of official reprisals if they surrendered. Finally, wherever there were guerrillas, there were political commissars who drilled the population in the parrot cries and slogans of Vietnamese Marxism. As soon as an area had been 'liberated' by the Communists, they set up their own administration, with their schools, tax collectors, and officials. French students described such organizations as 'parallel hierarchies'.

All this has to be seen against the theoretical background of Mao's books and, later, of Truong Chinh's and Vo Nguyen Giap's. In fact, of course, practice came before theory and the three men wrote their most important books while the fighting was on, as a way of rationalizing what they had been doing and providing a guide for action by lesser men.

Mao enshrined his doctrine in two essays: *Guerrilla Warfare* (1937) and *Strategic Problems of China's Revolutionary War* (1938), which have also been published under other titles. He envisaged a protracted war in three stages. During the first, the revolutionary forces would be weak and must preserve their strength, if necessary by retreating. Retreat, indeed, especially in a country as vast as China, led naturally to the second phase: the enemy's lines of communication, by this time, had been stretched to the limit and he had to stop to consolidate his gains. While he was doing this, the revolutionaries would do two things: harass the enemy with guerrilla action, and begin equipping a regular army for the third and final stage – that of the revolutionary final offensive. In this the enemy is surrounded by a hostile population thoroughly infiltrated by revolutionary guerrillas; his forces are exhausted and demoralized; and the revolutionary army has grown strong enough to move in for the kill.

In *The Resistance Will Win*, Truong Chinh goes along with Mao in distinguishing three phases of revolutionary war which, however, he restyles the stages of 'contention', 'equilibrium' and 'general counter-offensive'. The most important passages in his essay are those that deal with the political aspects of the first Indo-China war, and it is interesting to compare his political

61

arguments with Mao's. Neither Mao nor Truong Chinh said much about Communism and what it held in store for their respective peoples. Both made their primary appeal to the elemental force of *patriotism* – against the Japanese and the French. But there were important subsidiary appeals. The Chinese Communists promised the peasants they would all share in a redistribution of lands; they said nothing about the forced collectivization that was to follow. Similarly, Truong Chinh made utterly cynical promises, which, as the then Secretary-General of the Party, he well knew would never be honoured. Take, for instance, the following passage from *The Resistance Will Win*:

> At present, the French invaders are striving to deceive and divide our people. To sow discord between our Catholic and non-Catholic compatriots, they order their agents to (tell) the Catholic patriots that the Viet Minh are Communists. . . . They say that, later on if the impossible happened and the resistance was victorious, our Catholic compatriots would be forbidden to worship God, that the churches would be burnt and the crucifixes destroyed. . . .
> Such misleading propaganda must be brought to nothing. Communism is a doctrine that hides neither its end nor its means. But it is not our intention here to explain what Communism is. However, our Catholic compatriots should realize that the Ho Chi Minh government is a government of the entire people, approved by the National Assembly. This resistance war is a revolutionary war of the entire people led by our government. It is not a private war concerning only the Communists or the Viet Minh Front. The Communists or the Viet Minh Front have the sole aim of gaining freedom and independence for Vietnam. This resistance will bring democratic freedoms to our people, including freedom of belief and freedom of religion.

Giap, the military architect of the Communist victory, also paid close attention to political factors in his *La Guerre de la Libération et l'Armée Populaire* (1950), and again in his later collection of essays, *Guerre du Peuple, Armée du Peuple* (1961). Accepting Mao's three stages of revolutionary war, he elaborated the last. As Giap saw it, four conditions would have to be fulfilled before the final offensive could be launched. The people's army must have established absolute moral superiority in its own eyes and in that of the people; it must have improved its supplies and, in general, its material resources, the international situation would have to be favourable (he apparently had in mind the help the Viet Minh was getting from China and to a lesser degree from Russia); and finally, the people's army must have confidence in victory in the face of declining confidence on the enemy side. It will be seen that the fourth and first conditions are virtually the same, but no matter: Giap knew what he was about. His one error, as we have seen, was in trying to 'jump the gun' by launching a 'final offensive' at the beginning of 1951 before conditions were ripe.

Apart from his strategic insight, Giap was a masterly organizer. He had built up three separate but complementary army organizations: the regulars, the 'regionals', and the 'populars'. Until 1950, the largest Viet Minh regular army unit was the regiment, but at the end of the war, Giap commanded six divisions of some 9,500 men each, plus several regiments. The regional troops were, in effect, full-time guerrillas in the various provinces. The popular troops, attached to their own villages, were divided into auxiliaries of both sexes (who performed sabotage, intelligence, and supply duties), and part-time guerrillas. It was a fundamental characteristic of the first Indo-China war, especially in the Red River Delta, that the Vietnamese villager was a peasant by day and a soldier by night. Correspondingly, the French controlled only the major towns in any real sense; they controlled the countryside only superficially and in daylight – after dark, the Viet Minh took over. This is what the French meant when they talked of the *pourrissement* of the delta. By the time Dien Bien Phu had entered its death throes, the Viet Minh were everywhere and French control had become purely theoretical. The Americans and South Vietnamese were to undergo much the same painful experience ten years later.

Chapter Four

THE COMMUNIST INSURRECTIONS OF 1948

THE MASTER PLAN

Insurrections broke out almost simultaneously in the first half of 1948 in Burma, Malaya, Indonesia, and the Philippines. All were Communist-directed and this was not by coincidence: in fact, all these movements were part of a predetermined plan worked out in Moscow and Calcutta. Considered as a whole, they are of fundamental importance to an understanding of what is going on in South-East Asia today. Why, for instance, were these Communist-led insurrections unsuccessful, as they all were, whereas the anti-French insurrection in Vietnam, also Communist-led, ended in victory in 1954? Then again, why were the Malayan and Philippine uprisings successful in the early stages but defeated in the end, whereas the Indonesian one petered out very quickly and the Burmese one was never more than a wasteful nuisance? In other ways, too, the course of the insurrections of South-East Asia holds lessons for today. The difference between the Malayan and Indonesian experiences, for example, does much to explain the clash between the two countries over Malaysia.

I shall give short answers to my two questions, then fill in the facts that support my conclusions. Indeed I have already explained why the Communists won their victory in Vietnam, but if one leaves out such elements as Giap's talents and Chinese help, one is left with two basic facts. One is that the Vietnamese

Communists identified themselves with the nationalist movement and led it. The other is that the French refused to the last to give Vietnam the substance of independence. The French could probably have won the first Indo-China war, but not for themselves: for the non-Communist nationalists.

When we turn to the 1948 insurrections, we find that in the end they all failed because they were irrelevant to the people's needs or to the aspirations of the nationalists. The Philippines and Burma were both independent when the rebellions began. Indonesia had proclaimed its independence three years earlier but was still fighting the Dutch; the Indonesian people saw little reason why they should turn against their own leaders just because the Communists said they ought. As for Malaya, the Communists made headway when independence was not in sight but began to lose when the pace of constitutional advance was hastened. In the Philippines, also, as I have mentioned, the Communists enjoyed early successes, but this had nothing to do with independence, for the islands had been independent since 1946. What did have a lot to do with the Communist successes was the fact that independence had done nothing to improve the Philippine peasants' lot.

Let me now substantiate what I have written. First, the Communist conspiracy. We have seen how the earlier Communist attempts to seize power by violence, in Singapore, the Philippines, and elsewhere, ended in failure and frustration. For many years, the local Communists were in gaol or in hiding and Moscow refrained from encouraging open rebellion in Western colonial territories. The Second World War and its Asian sequels, however, changed the picture in ways which Communist theorists found difficult to square with their own theories. According to Lenin and Stalin, it was unthinkable that 'imperialists' should discard their colonies. Yet this is just what the Americans had done with the Philippines, and the British with India, Pakistan, Ceylon, and Burma. In Burma and the Philippines – two of the countries that concern us in this chapter – the Communists had failed to come to power although they had been in tactical alliance with the nationalists for anti-Japanese purposes. In Communist jargon, the situation in these countries was that 'bourgeois nationalist' régimes were in power. The national revolution in these countries was therefore incomplete and had to be 'completed' by the overthrow of the bourgeois nationalists. In the old days, this would have been a job for the Comintern, but this body had been formally dissolved during the war. In 1947, it was resurrected under a new name: the Cominform. In September of that year, the new body met in Poland and heard a momentous speech by Stalin's right-hand man, Zhdanov, who argued that the world had now split into two mutually hostile blocs. The time had now come, he said, for the colonial peoples 'to expel their oppressors'.

The new marching orders, for this is what they were, were transmitted to Communist parties throughout the world by the Cominform's journal, *For a Lasting Peace, for a People's Democracy*. But more precise instructions were needed. It is now known that these were given in Calcutta in February 1948, at an Asian Youth Conference sponsored by two Communist-controlled 'front' organizations, the World Federation of Democratic Youth and the International Union of Students. As soon as the Calcutta conference ended, its Communist participants from the countries that were 'to expel their oppressors' went home with Moscow's instructions. The detailed execution of marching orders, was, however, largely left to the individual Communist parties.

THE PLAN IN ACTION

It is illuminating to recall what happened in each country as the local parties got their orders. This means gathering up the threads as we left them two chapters back. In Burma, as we have seen, the nationalist and Communist leaders, Aung San and Thakin Soe, had collaborated, then quarrelled. In February 1946, Soe went further still and walked out of the Burmese Communist Party with his followers to set up a Communist party of his own, with pronounced Trotskyist tendencies – that is, while advocating revolution on Marxist and Leninist lines, it no longer considered itself bound by

Moscow's directives. The main Communist party, under Than Tun, remained in Aung San's AFPFL, but embarrassed it in all kinds of ways – by fomenting labour troubles, for instance, and by anti-government and anti-Buddhist propaganda at a time when the AFPFL was grooming itself as the party that would rule Burma – and all Burmans – after independence. In October 1946, Aung San had had enough and expelled the Communist party from the AFPFL. The violence of bandits, terrorists, and murderers had come to an end in many parts of Burma. Now, in 1947, Than Tun's Communists thought the time had come, with independence drawing near, to make their peace with the AFPFL. For a start, they pledged their help in stamping out banditry and terrorism. Then in October came the agreement between Clement Attlee and U Nu that paved the way for independence. The Communists, still on their good behaviour, welcomed it and declared their support for the interim government of Burma. This, you will notice, was shortly after Zhdanov's call to arms before the Cominform. But the news had probably not reached Than Tun at the time, and he seemed quite unaware that he was about to perform one of those spectacular somersaults that so characterize Communist parties, whether in power or in opposition. By 4 January 1948, when independence was proclaimed, Moscow's new line had reached the Burmese Communists and the somersault duly came. Three months earlier they had supported the Attlee–Nu agreement; now they denounced it and declared that Burma was being fobbed off with a false independence. By March, the Calcutta order must have reached the Burmese Communists, and at the end of the month they went into dissidence, calling themselves the White Flags. The Trotskyists were already fighting and had become known as the Red Flags. These, moreover, were only two of the insurrections that have plagued Burma since independence, for in addition to the ideological ones there were a number of separatist movements in which non-Burmese peoples, like the Karens, the Kachins, and the Shans, tried to win freedom from Burmese rule.

The *Philippine* situation was equally complex and fascinating. One complicating factor was an early symptom of the Sino-Soviet ideological squabble that provides food for thought in the light of more recent developments. The Filipino Communist Party had split into rival 'Russian' and 'Chinese' wings. The majority section, headed by Pedro Castro, followed the Moscow line which, at that time, advocated Communist participation in a coalition government that would agree to a more or less Marxist programme. The minority faction, headed by Castro's predecessor, Vicente Lava, who had been the party boss during the Japanese occupation, wanted to set up a People's Democratic government, using Mao Tse-tung's methods to achieve this aim. As we have seen, in the Philippines as elsewhere, the politicians had divided into 'collaborators' and 'resisters' during the Japanese period. The two groups fought it out in the elections of April 1946, which were being held, with American approval, in fulfilment of the United States pledge of independence for the Philippines. The anti-Japanese politicians were led by Sergio Osmeña and the collaborationists by Manuel Roxas. Neither of the Communist Party factions supported Roxas, but they were divided in their attitude towards Osmeña and his followers. The Castro majority, in line with Moscow, wanted to enter a government headed by Osmeña, the better to control it from within. The more militant Lava group wanted a showdown with Osmeña with the aim of forcing him to proclaim a 'people's' government. In the event, these rival calculations turned out to be irrelevant, for it was not Osmeña but the collaborationist Roxas who came out on top in the elections. The Moscow-line coalition plan was thus inapplicable and the Communist Party as a whole adopted the violent course which Lava's 'showdown' policy would have made inescapable anyway.

This is where Luis Taruc and the Huks once more came into their own. Theoretically, the Huks had been disbanded (see p. 42), but now, after the elections, Taruc gathered his followers around him and they dug up the arms they had hidden. Soon the Huks were in action again and President Roxas's inept attempts at suppression only served to swell their numbers and

enthusiasm. Early in 1948, when the Zhdanov line was beginning to be diffused among the Asian Communist Parties, the
Huks were in control of various rural districts in eastern and
central Luzon, the main island of the Philippines. Communication difficulties must have been particularly severe, for Taruc
(who had not told his followers he was a Communist) does not
appear to have heard of the Zhdanov–Calcutta line until mid-
April. If he had, it is hard to see why he should have done what he
did. In April President Roxas died suddenly and his successor,
President Quirino, called on the Huks to surrender their arms,
in return for a guaranteed amnesty. Taruc himself negotiated
with Quirino and accepted his terms. He had scarcely done so,
however, when he withdrew to the hills once more and resumed
fighting on a larger scale than before. It must be presumed that
Moscow's precise instructions reached him just after the
negotiations had been completed. And indeed he now decided
it was time to take off the mask he had consistently worn as the
champion of peasant rights. For the first time he revealed that
he was a Communist.

In *Indonesia*, too, the Communists turned a somersault, in
circumstances strikingly reminiscent of those in Burma. We
have already followed the career of Tan Malaka, the great
adventurer of the PKI (Partai Kommunis Indonesia) until the
time when the Japanese brought him to Java (see p. 38). He was
to have been their nominee for control of the Indonesian
nationalist movement from within. As it turned out, Tan Malaka
was nobody's nominee. He worked for himself, for private dreams
and ambitions that were never fulfilled. I have described him as
unscrupulous. Here is an example. He had a document drawn
up transferring all power to him in the event of the deaths of
President Sukarno and Vice-President Hatta, then forged their
signatures on it. He tried to talk the Socialist leader Sjahrir into
joining him in a *coup d'état*, to be followed immediately by the
expropriation of all foreign properties without compensation.
In preparation, he circulated rumours that Sukarno and Hatta
had been killed by the British, whose troops reached Indonesia
ahead of the Dutch after Japan's defeat. Had Sjahrir accepted

his proposal, he would have produced his forged document as a badge of legitimacy. But this time Tan had over-reached himself. Sjahrir refused and in March 1946 the Republican authorities had Tan gaoled.

Meanwhile other new names, notably those of Alimin, Musso, Jusuf, Sardjono and Sjarifuddin, had appeared among the Communist leaders. Most of these men had spent the war years abroad. Alimin, for instance, had been away for twenty years, first in Moscow, then in Yenan with the Chinese Communists; Musso had spent most of his time in Moscow and Sardjono had been in Australia.

One of them, Jusuf, was gaoled at the same time as Tan Malaka. After the Japanese defeat, he had set up the PKI again and used it to promote terrorist activities against Sukarno's government. This was a confused period. Jusuf's PKI was not the genuine article. Sardjono, the man who had been in Australia, came back to Indonesia about the time Jusuf was gaoled and, in May, he re-established the real PKI. Alimin, returning from Moscow, joined Sardjono and between them they scored an astonishing success of leadership and organization. When Japan collapsed, there had been no Communist Party in the true sense of the term and Communist influence was negligible; by 1948 the restored PKI had a large membership and, more important still, had gained control of the trade-union and youth movements. It was thus in a fairly strong position at the time of the Cominform and Calcutta conferences.

Here again, however, the Communists found themselves performing a policy somersault. The man principally involved was Sjarifuddin, who – like Taruc in the Philippines – was a crypto-Communist. Sjarifuddin's label was 'Socialist'. During the war, he had taken part in the small anti-Japanese resistance movement. In 1948, the year of insurrection, he was Indonesia's Prime Minister, working closely with the Socialist Sutan Sjahrir. On 7 January 1948, his cabinet reached a truce agreement with the Dutch, who had launched a 'police action' against the Indonesian Republic the previous July, with the object of recapturing the most valuable territories of their former colony. The agreement was named after the U.S. Navy transport *Renville*, on which it was signed. It was an unpopular agreement and it brought the Sjarifuddin cabinet down. Almost simultaneously, the Sjarifuddin–Sjahrir alliance fell apart, Sjarifuddin taking his hardcore of followers with him to organize a People's Democratic Front (*Front Demokrasi Rakjat*, or FDR) to work up mass support for the Communists (though he had still not revealed that he himself was one of them). This was in February and the new Front announced its support for the *Renville* agreement. In March, however, the delegates who had attended the Calcutta Youth Conference brought back Moscow's instructions, and Sjarifuddin's Front denounced the *Renville* agreement. Simultaneously, it called for the nationalization of all foreign properties without compensation. The somersault had been accomplished.

The Communists, however, though psychologically ready to obey Moscow's instructions, were not ready physically. Nor was Moscow satisfied with their leadership for military purposes, successful though it had been in the political sense. The Russians had picked their man: Musso, who had been in exile in Moscow. But a way had to be found to get Musso into Indonesia without arousing suspicion. This took time. Musso did not return until 12 August 1948, bearing a passport in the name of Suparto and representing himself as the secretary of a young Indonesian who had been to Prague on a diplomatic mission. This young man, whose name was Suripno, was also a Communist.

As soon as Musso was back, armed with precise orders from Moscow, he assumed the leadership of the PKI, set up headquarters at Madiun, in Java, and started a Red Army School. Dynamic though Musso was, he knew he would need months of preparation before launching his rebellion, for unlike the Communists in the Philippines and Malaya his followers didn't have a resistance army on which to build. Their military preparations had to be made from scratch. But in the event his *putsch* went off at half-cock, for some of his over-enthusiastic followers started anti-government disturbances that brought the Republican army marching on Madiun. Having no choice, Musso issued a 'call to arms' on 18 September. By that time, he had only three or four thousand armed men, indifferently trained. Within a fortnight the Communists had lost Madiun and on 25 October President Sukarno announced the crushing of the rebellion. Musso was killed in action and most of the PKI leaders – including Sjarifuddin, who had at last come into the open – were shot.

As if to add to the complications of a period of remarkable confusion, the irrepressible Tan Malaka, released from gaol on 16 September, only two days before Musso's call to arms, went on to form the Murba (proletariat) party – a nationalist Communist group that stood aloof from Soviet and Chinese affiliations, and dissociated itself from Musso's *putsch*. In no time, with his magnetic appeal, second only to Sukarno's, he had built up an enormous personal following. He might well, indeed, have ousted Sukarno and Hatta from power. But in April 1949 he was captured by the army; and on the 16th he was executed. It was an abrupt end to a remarkable career.

It is easy enough to see why the PKI's attempted insurrection had failed so ignominiously. It was not simply that the Communist army was small and ill-trained. The fundamental reason for its failure was that nobody was particularly interested in Musso's call to arms. In the eyes of the people, Sukarno and Hatta were the heroes of independence and the enemies were the Dutch. Now the Communists were calling on them to rise against their heroes. It didn't make sense. Writing his memoirs in prison Suripno, the young Communist who had returned from Prague with Musso as his 'secretary', put it succinctly: 'The lesson we learned, a very precious one, although very hard, was that the people did not support us.'

In *Malaya* too, the Communists had had their leadership troubles, though in simpler form than in Indonesia. In March 1947 the Secretary-General of the Malayan Communist Party disappeared with the party funds. He was a rather mysterious personage, called Loi Tak or Lai Tek, and thought to have been a Vietnamese. Into his shoes stepped Ch'in P'eng, the youthful veteran of the Malayan People's Anti-Japanese Army and recipient of the O.B.E. It is now known that the Malayan Communists, probably because of their close connexion with the Chinese Communist Party, had decided as early as 1946 to overthrow the government and set up a people's republic. As a prelude to action, they used their position within the trade-union movement to spark off a wave of strikes in 1947. Then came the Cominform, the Zhdanov line, and the Calcutta conference, which the Malayan Communists attended. Now the Russians and Chinese were in line and the hour of action had come. An Australian Communist leader, L. L. Sharkey, spent two weeks in Singapore on his way home from Calcutta and appears to have discussed the Malayan plan in detail.

It was a plan on the grand scale and inspired by Mao Tse-tung's model. The Malayan Communists envisaged an uprising in three stages. First, 'liberated areas' would be set up, to serve as recruiting bases. Then the liberated areas would be broadened; and finally the whole country would be 'liberated' by the merging of the Communist-held areas. To this end, Ch'in P'eng resurrected the old MPAJA under the more topical name of Malayan People's Anti-British Army. But at the end of 1949, when Mao's armies had triumphed in China, the Malayan Communists made another change, to Malayan Races' Liberation Army – a name that offered two advantages: it echoed Mao's 'People's Liberation Army', and it disguised the fact that the 'soldiers' under Ch'in P'eng's orders were nearly all Chinese.

COMMUNIST FAILURE IN THE
PHILIPPINES AND MALAYA

The Indonesian Communist rebellion (the Madiun affair, as it is usually called) was a non-starter, and so was the Burmese one, for although it dragged on and on its popular appeal was very limited. But this was not true of the Malayan and Filipino insurrections which, at the outset at least, had a very real chance of success. It is not necessary (nor indeed possible in a limited space) to describe either of them in detail. What interests us here is what happened in the end and why.

In both countries the Communists had spectacular early successes. This was due as much to the ineptness of the authorities as to the dramatic impact of the terrorist methods used by the Communists. In Malaya, the British were both unprepared for the scale and violence of the Communist attack and unwilling to take the action the situation demanded. In the Philippines, President Roxas had rashly boasted that he would wipe out the Huks in sixty days, but their movement snowballed and he was powerless to stop it.

But there were deeper and more positive reasons for the early Communist successes in both places. In Malaya, independence was not even in sight when the Emergency was proclaimed in June 1948. Ch'in P'eng and his followers seemed to be offering something to the Malayan Chinese who, broadly speaking, were kept out of the political race. And the Malays, though they did not support the insurrection, didn't feel themselves particularly involved in the fight against it either: what the British did was up to them. In the end, the tide was turned back by a combination of political and military-police action. The first was fundamental, the second indispensable. In point of time, the military-police action came first. The aim was to break the contact between the Communist Terrorists (as they were officially called) and the mainly Chinese villagers who provided them with food and information. This was done – first under General Sir Harold Briggs from 1950, then two years later under General Sir Gerald Templer – by resettling the Chinese squatters in 'New Villages' behind barbed wire, and by determined raids that drove the terrorists deeper and deeper into the jungle and eventually out of Malaya into Siam. By that time, in the late 1950s, the Communist 'army' had been reduced from a peak of about 8,000 to a few hundred stragglers.

On the political side, General Templer, arriving in Kuala Lumpur in February 1952 as High Commissioner, brought with him a plan for accelerated constitutional advance leading to independence. In time this plan, which was pushed with increasing vigour by Templer's successor, Sir Donald MacGillivray, took the wind out of the Communist sails. By good fortune, the Malays had thrown up a natural leader in Tunku Abdul Rahman. The Tunku's Alliance party, representing Malay and Chinese communal interests, won fifty-one of the fifty-two elected seats in Malaya's first general election in July

1955, and the Tunku himself was appointed Chief Minister. From that time, the Communists had nothing to offer and were morally defeated. Full independence within the Commonwealth came on 31 August 1957, with the Alliance government in power. Two years later, the Alliance – by this time reinforced by representatives of the Indian community – won another substantial electoral victory, being returned with seventy-four seats out of 104. In 1960 – three years after Malaya had achieved independence and twelve years after Ch'in P'eng had tried to carry out Zhdanov's orders – the Emergency was officially called off.

In the Philippines, the Communists couldn't appeal to nationalism, since independence had come two years before they took to the hills; but they could and did appeal to the deepest emotions of an oppressed peasantry. Nothing had ever been done for the Filipino peasants and nothing was being done now, in 1948. Absentee landlords were still growing fat on the proceeds of the peasants' crops and taxes; and in Manila, the Quirino administration was no better than that of the late President Roxas. In 1949, Quirino's political machine, in which armed men and money played a leading part, ensured his re-election. In 1950 official corruption was at its most flagrant and its evils were redoubled by falling copra prices and dwindling foreign exchange reserves. Public works programmes were halted and the salaries of officials fell months in arrears.

Against this background and that of a general collapse of faith in government, Taruc changed the name of the Hukbalahap to Hukbong Mapagpalaya ng Bayan (People's Liberation Army), much as in Malaya, and called for the overthrow of the Quirino administration. The new Huks demonstrated with humiliating ease that they were able at will to gain control not only of rice-bowl areas but even of provincial capitals in Luzon.

This was the situation in mid-1950. Yet a year later the Huks were on the run; in 1953, their military power was broken; and on 17 September 1954, Luis Taruc himself surrendered. It was an astonishing turning of the tables. How did it happen? The answer consists very largely of one name: Magsaysay: or two, if one includes the astute American adviser at his elbow, Colonel (later Brigadier-General) Lansdale. Congressman Ramón Magsaysay was appointed Defence Minister in September 1950, at a time when the Huks seemed on the point of carrying out their aim of overthrowing the central government. A month later, however, the army captured a number of leading Communist Party members in Manila, frustrating Huk plans for a take-over. Altogether 105 Communists were seized in these October raids, including the Secretary-General of the Party, José Lava, one of the brothers of Vicente Lava, whom we met earlier and who had since died.

Honest, forthright, and prodigiously energentic, Magsaysay moved into action under a programme of 'All-out force and all-out friendship'. Convinced that the great majority of Taruc's followers were not Communists at heart, he set out to win them over. He set up a rural rehabilitation programme for Huks who responded to his call and surrendered. If they had not been guilty of certain specified crimes, he saw to it that they got land and a loan of money to put it to use. He cleaned out the army and constabulary of dead wood and the corrupt, and had peasants defended by army lawyers against the landlords who tried to prosecute them. He was everywhere, indefatigable – and like other dynamic leaders, de Lattre and Templer, he galvanized the whole country, and rallied enemies to his own banner. It was a remarkable achievement, and it swept him into power as President of the Philippines in the 1953 elections. His death in an air crash in March 1957 was a tragedy for the Filipinos. His life had shown that it was possible to defeat the Communists by removing the grievances on which their appeal rested.

It does not detract from Magsaysay's achievement to record that the Huk threat started reviving in 1966 and 1967. Feeding, as before, on land grievances and poverty, the new Huks, led by Faustino Delmundo – alias Commander Sumolong – controlled about half a million people in 1,400 square miles of Central Luzon by the spring of 1967. President Marcos, despite an ambitious civic action programme, seemed unable to arrest spreading lawlessness, of which Huk terrorism was only a part.

Part Three OUTSIDE PRESSURES

Chapter One CHINA

We have seen how dramatically the Communist victory in the Chinese civil war affected the military situation in what was then French Indo-China. In this and in many other ways, 1949 was a turning point in Asia. There are two major reasons why Mao Tse-tung's victory was of supreme importance. One is that for the first time after a century of wars and revolutionary upheaval, a central government imposed its will over the remotest parts of its realm, uniting a country with an ancient history and the most numerous and self-confident people on earth. The other reason was that not merely were China's new rulers Communists – and therefore hostile to the non-Communist world as a whole – but they were a very special brand of Communists who put Communism unreservedly in the service of China's national ambitions.

China must, however, even under the Communists, be seen in proportion. Unified though it soon was under Mao's rule, it was not, in absolute terms, a great power. By this, I mean that it did not dispose of military fire-power to compare with Russia's or America's or even Britain's. Even today, after years of prodigious, directed efforts to industrialize itself, it lacks the industrial base to sustain a war against any one of the nuclear powers. But in a regional and relative sense, China *is* a great power and already was in 1950. It had shown its determination to restore the frontiers of imperial China by invading Tibet in

October 1950. A few weeks later, it intervened on the Communist side in the Korean War and, by fighting the United Nations forces to a standstill, proved it was a military power of some magnitude, which none of its neighbours could ignore. From Afghanistan to Korea, China's neighbours knew in their hearts that they could not stand up to the Chinese military machine. Moreover, in another sense, made real by China's size and numbers, it *was* a great power. For was there another power on earth that could hope to occupy and control China in any but a very transient sense ?

There has been much argument over Communist China's military intentions and the supposed aggressiveness of its leadership. But it all depends, as C. E. M. Joad would have said, on what you mean by aggressiveness, or aggression. Certainly the Chinese People's Republic is a *militant* régime, ready to use force to settle an international argument its own way. It does not follow that it is an aggressive and expansionist power in the way Hitler's Germany was. On the other hand, it could be argued that the Chinese Communists have refrained from overrunning the whole of South-East Asia only because of the daunting protective umbrella the United States has thrown over that region. Since the American military presence is a fact, and so is China's military restraint in South-East Asia, it is impossible to settle the argument.

There are, in fact, very few certainties about Peking's foreign policy. One is that the Chinese Communists consider the United States to be China's principal enemy. It is clear enough that Peking would like the Americans out of Formosa, South Vietnam, and Laos; this much the Chinese Communists have said many times. Beyond that, nearly everything is speculation.

In practice the Chinese Communists have blown hot and cold in their diplomatic relations with other Asian countries. The harder phases have seemed to coincide with periods of tension either within China, or in China's relations with Russia, or both. It is no surprise that the first phase, beginning in 1949, was an intransigent one, for it coincided with the full rigour of a triumphant revolution at home. In November 1949, shortly after the proclamation of the Chinese People's Republic, Liu

Shao Ch'i, who stood next to Mao in the Party leadership, declared ominously:

The path taken by the Chinese people in defeating imperialism and its lackeys and in founding the Chinese People's Republic is the path that should be taken by the peoples of the various colonial and semi-colonial countries in their fight for national independence and people's democracy.

The Chinese Communists have never abandoned this insistence on the violent path to power. But during the 'soft' phases of their diplomacy, they have kept it out of sight in places where it might cause offence. Between 1949 and 1954, however, they were not at all concerned whether or not they were going to offend people. At home, they were executing landlords, spies, bandits, and reactionaries, as they put it; abroad, or at least beyond the boundaries of China proper, they were militarily involved in Tibet and Korea. While all this was going on they had little interest in soft words or deeds in Asia or elsewhere. Liu's call for violence was a guiding policy and Peking's interest lay in subverting neighbouring governments, not helping them. In Malaya, the Philippines, and Vietnam, especially, they found their opportunities.

After the Korean armistice (July 1953) and the French defeat in Indo-China the following spring, the Chinese Communists began to see advantages in cultivating a more neighbourly image. The first sign of a change came during the Far Eastern conference at Geneva in 1954, which brought the first Indo-China war to an end. This was a big occasion for the Chinese Communists. Except for the Korean truce talks at Panmunjom, this was the first East–West conference they had attended. In a sense, it was their diplomatic début and they took full advantage of it. The smell of a Communist victory in Indo-China was already in the air in Geneva when the Chinese Foreign Minister, Mr Chou En-lai, arrived there on 25 April. The conference began four days later, but started off with procedural wrangles and an abortive discussion of the Korean question. It didn't settle down to its Indo-China phase till 8 May; and Dien Bien Phu had fallen the day before. Mr Chou, as the representative of a government whose help had made the Viet Minh victory possible, could therefore afford to appear magnanimous. He soon showed he could be. The conference had got bogged down because the Vietnamese Communist delegate, Pham Van Dong, was insisting that the Communist 'governments' the Viet Minh had set up in Laos and Cambodia should be recognized *de facto* for negotiating purposes. Now, on 16 June, Chou En-lai blandly swept aside this demand from a fellow-Communist by proposing bilateral talks between the Viet Minh and the (legitimate) governments of Cambodia and Laos, followed by the evacuation of all foreign troops from both countries. This broke the deadlock.

This was Communist China's reasonable face. On 29 April, the day the Geneva conference opened, the Chinese were giving another display of sweet reasonableness in Peking itself. Plenipotentiaries of India and China signed an agreement innocuously described as 'on trade and intercourse between the Tibet region of China and India'. This agreement has two titles to fame. One is that under it India recognized Tibet as part of China. The other is that it began with the first statement of the Panch Sila, or five principles of peaceful coexistence. Though these sound quaint enough in the light of later events along the Sino-Indian border, they have probably deceived more people in more places than any other document since the Second World War, and are therefore worth requoting here:

1. Mutual respect for each other's territorial integrity and sovereignty.
2. Mutual non-aggression.
3. Mutual non-interference in each other's internal affairs.
4. Equality and mutual benefit.
5. Peaceful coexistence.

In June, during a lull in the Geneva conference, Mr Chou flew to Delhi, where he and Mr Nehru publicly reaffirmed the five principles. It was logical enough for Chou En-lai to be chosen as the standard-bearer of China's more amiable visage, not merely because he was Foreign Minister as well as Prime Minister, but because his personality fitted the role. His handsome, bushy-eyebrowed presence, his ease of manner and cosmopolitan background (he studied in France and Germany), were ideal. These assets were again in evidence in April 1955 during the Afro-Asian conference at Bandung. This, too, was an important occasion for China. The Soviet Union, although most of its area lies in Asia, had not been invited to Bandung, so that China was the major representative of the Communist world. By this time, Mao Tse-tung's régime had emerged from its worst teething troubles. In Korea and at Geneva it had demonstrated that China was again a great power. Now it was bent on effacing the militarist associations of Tibet and Korea by showing itself as a *peace-loving* power. And not merely peace-loving, but *Asian* (unlike Russia).

Unfailingly suave and unruffled, Chou En-lai put up a brilliant performance at Bandung. The real trouble in Asia, he said, was not Chinese subversion but the establishment of bases around China. Then, as if to prove China's goodwill, he took advantage of his presence on Indonesian soil to sign an agreement with the Indonesian government on the status of Indonesia's large Chinese minority.

This softer phase of Peking's diplomacy ended towards the close of 1957. The previous year had brought, in dramatic succession, Mr Khrushchev's denunciation of Stalin and the Polish and Hungarian revolutions. The first tentative thaw had bewildered Communist parties everywhere and freedom's taste had proved too heady. At home, in 1957, Mao Tse-tung had initiated a thaw of his own, the famous 'Hundred Flowers' episode, 'Let one hundred flowers bloom, let one hundred schools of thought contend,' he had said poetically, and the suppressed intellectuals – scholars and professors, journalists and students – claimed their new freedom of speech with a gusto that surprised, then terrified, the Chinese Communist Party. In June, the party clamped down on the intellectuals, executing, for a start, the ringleaders of a students' riot. The 'hundred flowers' had been in bloom for only six weeks. In November, the twelve ruling Communist parties gathered in Moscow and issued a joint declaration denouncing 'revisionism' in terms of uncompromising violence. Mao himself was in the forefront of those who denounced the 'revisionists'. It was the end of the thaw – or at any rate a halt to it – and the fading of China's smile on the outer world.

The third phase of Chinese Communist diplomacy might be described as a selective return to the hard line of the early revolutionary years – selective because Mr Chou, ageing but still urbane, continued to smile at neighbouring Prime Ministers, especially if they were unattached to the West or showed a tendency to make anti-Western speeches. Prince Sihanouk of Cambodia has been ready to oblige in this respect and is always sure of a red carpet welcome in Peking.

Though Peking continued to pay lip service to 'peaceful coexistence', there was an increasing emphasis on violent revolution, and events within the Communist world aggravated this tendency. In China itself the tremendous effort to step up the pace of industrialization, known as the 'great leap forward', launched in 1958, had ended in frustration; and successive bad harvests created a serious food shortage in the next three years. In 1959, the cracks on the surface of Sino-Soviet friendship were beginning to be visible; and in 1960, the Russians withdrew their technicians from China. This was primarily a dispute between the two great powers of the Communist world over fundamental national policies, but it took an ideological form, so that the Chinese felt compelled to demonstrate their distinctness from the 'revisionist' Russians by continuing stress on the need for revolution, for instance in the countries of South-East Asia. On another front, the honeymoon with India was turning sour. In 1959, Tibet erupted in rebellion and Tibetan refugees, including the Dalai Lama, poured into India. Frontier incidents multiplied and in 1962 the Chinese army struck at India across contested territory in the Himalayas, routing the unprepared Indians.

Though these events only indirectly concern us here, they form the background to the general intransigence displayed by the Chinese Communists since 1957. Perhaps the most striking example of it that is directly relevant to our purposes was the behaviour of the Chinese delegation at the international conference on Laos, which began in April 1961 but did not end until July of the following year. The Chinese, led by Marshal

Ch'en Yi, the Foreign Minister, went there with the clear intention of going into battle against the United States. It would not be untrue to say that the conference was indeed a battlefield in the cold war. In the 1954 Geneva conference, the military position of the 'Western side' had sharply deteriorated shortly after the talking had begun. And this had a direct bearing on the 'concession' the Communist negotiators then felt prepared to make. The same thing happened during the Laos conference, but the deterioration took longer to develop, and so did the Communists' willingness to make 'concessions' – that is, to retreat from extreme demands made earlier. During the first few months of the conference, the Chinese delegates – in contrast with the Soviet ones – seemed more concerned to make vituperative speeches against the United States than to offer or consider constructive proposals. They became more 'reasonable' only after the American-supported forces in Laos had been routed.

More recently still, there has been a further sharp deterioration in China's relations with the outside world. On 3 September 1965, Marshal Lin Piao, Defence Minister and vice-chairman of the Politburo, launched an expanded version of Mao Tse-tung's theories of revolutionary war which seemed to bring the whole world under threat. In an article published that day, the Marshal – a military hero for his victories against the Japanese, Chiang Kai-shek's troops and the United Nations' forces in Korea – attempted to apply Mao's theory of 'encirclement of the cities from the countryside' to the whole world. On a world scale, he explained, the 'cities' were the capitalist countries, and the 'countryside' was the underdeveloped world of Asia, Africa and Latin America. 'Encirclement', however, could only be carried out by 'peoples' wars' led by Communists taking China's own revolutionary war as a model and eschewing Moscow's advice.

It is now clear that this curious theory, with its undertones of 'China against the world', was a preliminary attack in what has since come into the open as a far-reaching, but confused, struggle for power in China itself. The struggle itself was formally launched at the end of April 1966 under the fanciful name of 'great proletarian cultural revolution'. Although initially a campaign against intellectuals accused of propagating 'feudal', 'bourgeois' or 'revisionist' ideas, it soon emerged that it was about fundamental issues, in particular the succession to Mao, the nature of the revolution and its permanance, and even China's relations with the outside world, including the other Communist countries. And indeed all these themes were ultimately related.

Mao was 72 when the cultural revolution was launched. The form it took and the excesses the Chinese leader encouraged, must cast serious doubts on his sanity. The preservation for generations to come of the Chinese revolution – *his* revolution – had become an obsession. For the sake of revolutionary nationalism, he had quarrelled with Khrushchev and deprived China of Soviet aid. Now, for the sake of winning China's youth, he was willing to sacrifice the country's chances of economic development and educational progress. Not unnaturally, Lin Piao now emerged as Mao's Number Two – perhaps his successor. Egged on by Lin and Chiang Ching, Mao's wife, gangs of youths, known as 'Red Guards', were encouraged to molest Communist Party officials, frog-marching them through the streets, placing dunce's caps on their heads and in other ways humiliating them.

The accompanying purge removed a number of leading Chinese Communists and threatened others, including President Liu Shao-ch'i, who – in official ratings published in August 1966 – dropped from first position (after Mao) to seventh in the the party hierarchy. His place was taken by Lin Piao; the durable Chou En-lai, who publicly sided with Mao while trying to restrain the excesses of the Red Guards, remained as Number Two (after Lin).

Early in 1968, it was still impossible to predict the final outcome of the struggle, which was essentially one between Mao and his allies, including the mob, on the one hand, and on the other, Liu Shao-ch'i and the Communist Party. The Red Guards controlled most of the major cities, but there had been armed clashes between Maoists and anti-Maoists in various areas. Opposition to Mao was stiffest in the south-western provinces of Szechuan, Yunnan and Kweichow, and in the borderlands of Sinkiang, Inner Mongolia and Tibet.

During the whole period starting with Lin Piao's article in September 1965, China's relations with the outside world went from bad to worse. In Africa, several Chinese missions were expelled. In China itself, the Red Guards took to manhandling foreign diplomats, including Russians and Britons. The collapse of the Communist-supported coup in Djakarta in September and October 1965 – which Peking had supported – was followed by a sharp decline in China's relations with Indonesia, once a friend. Against this background of hooliganism and incipient civil war, China's prestige and influence declined drastically.

Although Peking continued to call for revolutionary action in South-East Asia, there was remarkably little evidence of *direct* Chinese involvement in the so-called 'liberation' movements in the area. The Chinese exhorted the North Vietnamese to fight American 'imperialism' to the bitter end, but seemed content to leave the actual fighting to the Vietnamese (threatening to intervene only if the Americans invaded North Vietnam). China's military involvement was limited to the provision of railway engineers to keep rail communications between North Vietnam and China open, and anti-aircraft troops to protect them – some 40,000 men in all.

It should be added that China had relatively little need to intervene directly in much of South-East Asia. In Vietnam, Laos and Cambodia, the Vietnamese Communists do all the subverting that needs to be done. In Burma, Malaysia, Singapore and the Philippines, Peking-orientated Communist parties or organizations do China's bidding. This is also true of Siam, where the membership of the small and illegal Communist Party of Thailand consists largely of Thais of Chinese origin who have spent long periods in China. China is, in fact, behind the terrorists who started activities in Siam in 1965 (though the Vietnamese and Laotian Communists are also involved). Operating mainly in the jungle areas near the Laotian border, the terrorists have kept up their pressure, forcing the Siamese to raise a force of 80,000 volunteers to fight them, and to spend about £10 million a year in security measures.

Chapter Two

SEATO AND AMERICAN INTERVENTION

AMERICAN POLICY

During the Second World War, President Roosevelt's Far Eastern policy was dominated by an obsessive determination to prevent the European allies of the United States from restoring their imperial positions. In this he was in agreement with Stalin; but not, of course, with Winston Churchill and still less with Charles de Gaulle. This attitude was reflected in precise instructions to American commanders in the area to withhold all help from the French in Indo-China. As we saw in an earlier chapter, the outcome of this coincidence of views between the anti-imperialist Americans and Communists was a period of warm relations between American agents and the Viet Minh and the curious episode which I have called the 'war of the intelligence services', in which the Americans and French were the antagonists.

Though Roosevelt is long dead, the ripples left by his Far Eastern policies are still spreading twenty years after. They can be seen through the lengthening history of American involvement in Indo-China until and including the clash between General de Gaulle and President Johnson in 1964 over the future of Vietnam, with which we shall deal when the time comes. Certainly the hand of the late F.D.R. can be clearly seen in the *manner* of Washington's decision to intervene on France's side in the first Indo-China war. The real reason for this decision was certainly the arrival of Mao Tse-tung's forces on the borders of Tonking. The Americans rightly foresaw that the Chinese Communists would soon be helping their Vietnamese friends. They were, however, faced with the fact that the French – fighting a colonial war of which they (the Americans) disapproved – were also fighting Communists who, moreover, were in a *de facto* alliance with the arch-enemy of the United States, Communist China. On anti-Communist grounds, the French qualified for American military aid; but the Americans were desperately anxious not to be identified with a colonial cause.

The United States had given diplomatic recognition on 7 February 1950 to Vietnam, Laos, and Cambodia, despite the limitations which their membership of the French Union imposed on their independence. Before the end of the month, France requested military and economic aid from the United States. The Americans were not unwilling, but would have liked the aid to go straight to the governments concerned, principally Bao Dai's. Hearing of this, the then commander-in-chief of the French forces in Indo-China, General Carpentier, said he would resign within twenty-four hours if the military aid went to the Vietnamese, though he was less concerned about the economic aid.

In the event, the military aid did go to the French authorities, which was logical enough as the Vietnamese still had no army of their own. But the American government took its time in thinking the matter over; and when, on 8 May, Mr Dean Acheson, the Secretary of State, announced that aid was to be made available to Vietnam, Laos, and Cambodia, he was careful to underline that its purpose was not to help French colonial ambitions.

On 25 June, the Soviet-trained North Korean army invaded South Korea, and two days later President Truman announced 'acceleration in the furnishing of military assistance to the forces of France and the Associated States in Indo-China and the dispatch of a military mission to provide close working relations with those forces'. This military mission, known as the Military Assistance Advisory Group, or MAAG, arrived in

89

Saigon in August 1950. This marked the real beginning of the American involvement in the Indo-China conflict.

At the outset, and indeed until the advent of President Kennedy in January 1961, successive American administrations tended to look at Far Eastern and South-East Asia in broad, simple generalities. Communism is bad; so is colonialism. Nationalism is good. Therefore true nationalists are anti-colonialist and anti-Communist. This was roughly how the American official assumptions ran; and indeed one of the compelling virtues of such simplicities is that they appeal to voters. This is important to politicians seeking Congressional support for costly military assistance programmes; and in the early days of the American involvement in Indo-China, the argument I have quoted had the additional merit of deflecting the wrath of that dangerous demagogue and witch-hunter, the late Senator Joseph McCarthy.

Holding such assumptions, the governments of Presidents Truman and Eisenhower devoted much time, energy, and money to the search for true nationalists in South-East Asia, and above all to the search for the right 'strong man', the charismatic figure capable of attracting support to himself and away from the Communists. Now in countries with short acquaintances of democracy and lengthy traditions of despotism, the search for a strong man makes sense. But the assumptions behind United States policy failed to take account of the complexities and perverseness of human nature, especially, perhaps, in the Far East. For example, the proposition that nationalists are against colonialism may be self-evident, but the anti-colonial Americans failed to understand that they themselves would come to be regarded as imperialists as soon as the extent of American involvement came to be generally known. Nor did they understand that neutralism or non-involvement is often an expression of nationalism and of newly-found independence (the late Mr John Foster Dulles who, as Secretary of State, played a dominant part in shaping Washington's Far Eastern policies, had gone so far as to say neutralism was 'immoral'). They therefore tended to lump neutralists and Communists together and were pained and astonished when leaders like Prince Sihanouk of

Cambodia, or U Nu or Ne Win of Burma, developed pronounced anti-American views.

Then the Americans, by and large, failed to grasp a disconcerting and indeed disturbing fact: that the same man can sometimes be both a Communist and a nationalist. This, though it ran utterly counter to American official doctrine, is true of Mao Tse-tung and Ho Chi Minh – two of the Far Eastern leaders who have brought maximum discomfiture to the United States, and to the West as a whole. One last point should be added to this list of shortcomings: a strong tendency, arising out of the colonial origins of the United States, to think that the European colonial powers are, by definition, wrong in everything that pertains to their dependencies or ex-dependencies. In fairness to the Americans, many of whose officials are men of the highest intellectual capacity, this sweeping view was considerably attenuated in Britain's case in the light of the British decolonization in Asia. But it has coloured Washington's entire relationship with the Indo-Chinese States and Indonesia.

In its search for local 'strong men', the United States used anti-Communism as a decisive credential, at least in the Dulles era. Administrative capacity, and even honesty, were less important than unwavering anti-Communism *plus* willingness to become a partner of the United States. Nor did it matter if a strong man was also an oppressive despot, as Syngman Rhee of Korea and Ngo Dinh Diem of Vietnam turned out to be, so long as he kept on repeating that he was anti-Communist. This alone was enough to qualify them as leaders of the 'free world', whatever their views on freedom within their own countries. On this basis, the American search for reliable strong men was seared with disappointments, with one notable exception: Magsaysay of the Philippines, who came to the fore through his own virtues and whom the Americans were able to help to great effect because his country, which had been their colony, was the only one in South-East Asia of which they had first-hand experience.

VIETNAM SINCE 1954

In South Vietnam, they thought they had found their man in Ngo Dinh Diem, whom we have met briefly as the stubborn Minister of the Interior in Bao Dai's first government under French rule. Stubborn, Mr Diem certainly was: he had refused to take office for more than twenty years because the French were still running Vietnam. But stubbornness, as the Americans soon found out, can be a two-edged weapon; and in the end, in November 1963, they were not sorry when a military *junta* overthrew him.

Strictly speaking, however, the Americans didn't *find* Ngo Dinh Diem. But they did give him unconditional support for years, in circumstances which we should now retrace.

The Geneva conference of 1954 had ended, on a rather theatrical note, on 21 July, with the clock stopped in the Palais des Nations to enable M. Mendès-France, the French Prime Minister, to say he had kept his undertaking to the National Assembly to bring peace back to Indo-China within a month of taking office, or resign. Given the military situation, as I have described it, the conference had not gone as badly as it might have, from a Western point of view, or at any rate from a French one. Cambodia came off best in that its territory was to be entirely cleared not only of Vietnamese and French troops but also of the so-called 'Khmer Resistance Forces' under those real and mythical scourges of the kingdom, Son Ngoc Thanh and Son Ngoc Minh. There were no ifs or buts. Laos did not fare quite so well. The national territory was left intact, at least in theory, but 'pending a political settlement', as the cease-fire agreement put it, the Communist-led Pathet Lao forces were to be concentrated in the two northern provinces they had long controlled with Viet Minh help: Sam Neua and Phong Saly. But the 'political settlement' proved elusive and, as we shall see, the Pathet Lao proved hard to dislodge. The Viet Minh was to withdraw its forces, piously known as 'Vietnamese People's Volunteer Forces', and the French theirs, apart from up to 1,500 commissioned and non-commissioned officers who were allowed to stay behind to train the Laotian army.

Vietnam, as might have been expected, fared worst of all. It was to be divided into two roughly equal halves along the 17th parallel, which truncates Annam (central Vietnam) at its narrowest point. All French forces were to be evacuated from North Vietnam, and all North Vietnamese troops were to quit the south.

So far, we have been considering the military cease-fire agreements signed by the enemy commands. Broadly speaking, these were honoured within the time-limits set. But the so-called 'Geneva agreements', as they are loosely called, included a number of unilateral declarations, and a 'final declaration', which was supposed to represent the concensus of the conference, but which was unsigned and therefore not, strictly speaking, binding on the participants. This final declaration included a clause calling for 'free elections' throughout Vietnam in July 1956, leading, by implication, to the reunification of the divided country. Now the United States and South Vietnamese delegations made statements explicitly dissociating themselves from certain aspects of the agreements; though the American chief delegate, Lieutenant-General Bedell Smith, declared that the United States would 'refrain from the threat or the use of force' to prevent their implementation. In fact, the provision for 'free elections' was never carried out.

Why did the Vietnamese and Americans take this stand? Let us look at the Vietnamese side first. Few people took much notice when, on 4 June 1954, French and Vietnamese representatives initialled agreements under which France, at last, recognized the independence of Vietnam. Independence had indeed come very late in the day, after the fall of Dien Bien Phu and while the delegates at Geneva were preparing to cut Vietnam in two. The Communists were victorious and the country was devastated, but the French were leaving. Who would be prepared to take over in such circumstances? Rumour had it that it would be Ngo Dinh Diem, who had been in Paris for the past few weeks after four years in exile, which he had spent mainly in the United States. This stay in America, during which he aroused the interest and support of the influential Cardinal Spellman, seems to have been a decisive factor in his appointment.

This, it should be noted, was up to Bao Dai as Chief of State. It was obvious enough to Bao Dai and everybody else, including the French, that whoever set out to save anything from the wreckage of non-Communist Vietnam would need American support. So Bao Dai made the appointment, dismissing objections from advisers who hinted – rightly as it turned out – that Diem would be disloyal to him. This was on 19 June; and on the 24th, Diem, who was virtually unknown in Cochinchina, arrived almost unnoticed in Saigon to take over his duties. He had scarcely formed his government when the Geneva conference entered its final phase. As a government, it had nothing to do with the war that was now lost, or with the peace that was depriving it of half its territory. In the circumstances, it is hardly surprising that it should dissociate itself from the agreements.

On the American side, the turn of events had been a bitter disappointment. It had been a plank of Mr John Foster Dulles's policy that Communism should be halted. Though the United States had kept only a small military mission in Vietnam and left the conduct of the war to the French, it had poured a good deal of money into the war effort.* Among the American politicians and military leaders were many who were deter-

* How much money is a matter of hot dispute among experts. Ellen J. Hammer, on page 313 of *The Struggle for Indo-China* (Stanford, 1954), quotes French official figures saying that in 1954 the American share of Indo-China war expenditure was running at 78·25 per cent. Dr Hammer is an American. The late Bernard B. Fall, a French Professor in an American university, wrote in a footnote on page 308 of *Street without Joy* (Pall Mall, 1963): 'To lay at rest once and for all the myth of the "American taxpayer financing the French in Indo-China": U.S. actual expenditures in Indo-China had reached an approximate total of $954 million by July 1954. During 1946–54, the French had spent close to $11 billion of their own funds for the prosecution of the war.' Allan B. Cole, in *Conflict in Indo-China 1945–1955* (Cornell, 1956), quotes quite different figures. I myself was told by Jean Letourneau, then French High Commissioner in Indo-China, in an interview published by the *Straits Times* on 14 July 1952, that 'American aid will now form fifty per cent of the total of military material being used in the war in Indo-China'. This proportion certainly went well beyond fifty per cent in the later stages of the war; but French expenditures included soldiers' pay and many other items beside military material.

mined that 'the Communists', who had humiliated the West in Korea, should not be allowed to get away with it again in Indo-China. On 7 April, a month before Dien Bien Phu fell, President Eisenhower himself, speaking as military man as much as Chief Executive, declared: 'The loss of Indo-China will cause the fall of South-East Asia like a set of dominoes' – an image that has remained a valid statement of U.S. policy. Four days later, Mr Dulles turned up in London, where he tried to talk Anthony Eden, the then British Foreign Secretary, into committing Britain to supporting American air–naval intervention to save Dien Bien Phu. One form of attack envisaged the use of an atomic bomb. But this plan, which has aroused a good deal of controversy ever since it was first proposed, came to nothing.

It was thus in a mood of frustration and defiance that the Americans took their places at the Geneva conference table. By the time the talks were ending, American policy rested on the firm determination to halt the advance of Communism in Vietnam. Hence General Bedell Smith's unilateral declaration. As yet, however, the Americans had not committed themselves with equal firmness to Ngo Dinh Diem. This did not come until the autumn, after Senator Mike Mansfield had visited Vietnam, Cambodia, and Laos on behalf of the Senate Committee on Foreign Relations. Senator Mansfield, in his report, recommended that United States economic aid should be extended to South Vietnam, but only if Ngo Dinh Diem stayed in office. On 25 October (still in 1954), President Eisenhower, in a letter to Diem, offered direct aid to his government (instead of aid channelled through France) in order, as he put it, to develop a strong State capable of resisting subversion and aggression. In what was to be the first of a long line of forlorn pleas, the President expressed the hope that the Diem government, in its turn, would carry out 'indispensable reforms'. Three weeks later, on 17 November, the President's personal ambassador to Vietnam, General Lawton F. Collins, arrived in Saigon and said American aid would henceforth be given only to Diem's government. By that time, the Vietnamese army was almost in open rebellion and General Collins added, significantly and effectively, that only an army faithful to its government would receive aid.

If the Geneva conference marked the end of the first phase of American intervention in Vietnam, the declarations of Mansfield, Eisenhower, and Collins may be said to have ushered in the second phase. From this point forward, the United States began to replace France as the dominant influence in South Vietnam. On 29 December 1954, Vietnam, Cambodia, and Laos broke away from the franc zone and gained the right to issue their own currencies; thereafter, Vietnam began to receive American aid direct in dollars instead of in francs through France, as had been the case. On the military side, the U.S. advisory mission, under General John W. O'Daniel, gradually took over the training of the South Vietnamese army from the French. On the political side, the shrewd and mysterious Colonel Lansdale, whom we have already met in connexion with President Magsaysay of the Philippines, moved into Mr Diem's palace and was at his elbow with advice during some of the challenges to his authority which he survived during his first year in office. On the administrative side, Michigan State University sent a team to Vietnam, under Professor Wesley R. Fishel, to offer advice on modernization.

This second phase of American policy was thus marked by a far deeper and more personal involvement than the first. A third phase, however, began towards the end of 1961, and for the first time the Americans found themselves involved in actual combatant operations in Vietnam. By this time the second Indo-China war was in full swing. It had begun quietly – while no one was looking, as it were – in 1958, with murders of provincial officials loyal to the Diem government. In January 1961, the Vietnamese Communists set up a 'National Front for the Liberation of South Vietnam'; by the end of the year, some 20,000 guerrillas were under arms and making rapid gains at the expense of the Southern government. In October, the Kennedy administration took alarm and sent a powerful mission, headed by General Maxwell Taylor, to Saigon to look at the problem and see what was needed. The Taylor report was kept secret, but it is known to have recommended greatly increased military aid to the Diem forces. On 8 February 1962, the United States set up a Vietnam command under General Paul D. Harkins. During the next few months, the American military establish-

ment in Vietnam was built up from not more than 5,000 men to
some 15,000. Though their instructions were to fire only when
fired upon, American soldiers and airmen were increasingly
involved in the actual fighting, and suffered casualties.

Relations between the Americans and the increasingly auto-
cratic Diem régime had become strained. It was a curious régime,
a family despotism with overtones of Renaissance intrigue.
Diem's eldest brother had been murdered by the Viet Minh,
but the brothers who were left formed a remarkable group. The
youngest and in some respects the ablest, Luyen, was sent to
London as ambassador. The eldest, Mgr Ngo Dinh Thuc, who
had been a bishop, became Archbishop of Hué in central
Vietnam. Can, a more distasteful character, was made Governor
of the centre (that is, the northern part of South Vietnam),
which he ruled with a ruthless hand. But perhaps the most important of the brothers was Nhu who, in some respects, was
more important than Diem himself. A born intriguer, addicted
to conspiratorial methods, Nhu was the *éminence grise* of the
régime. Officially, his title was Supreme Adviser to the President.
But he controlled the secret police, the Special Forces (used for
security and clandestine operations and financed by the American Central Intelligence Agency), the ruling National Revolutionary Movement, the Can Lao (Personality of the Worker) –
a kind of secret society within the National Revolutionary
Movement – the Republican Youth and the government-
sponsored trade-union body known as the Revolutionary Labour
Party. He introduced Personalism, a vague, authoritarian State
doctrine which purported to blend Catholic and Confucian
ideas. His wife, the attractive and formidable Madame Nhu,
was officially 'first lady', Diem being a bachelor. A fierce
feminist and moralist, she introduced laws banning divorce,
adultery, polygamy, prostitution, birth control, dancing, and
other misdeeds.

Diem had deposed Bao Dai in October 1955 in a referendum
that was controlled and managed from start to finish. Soon,
everybody who was anybody was found to be related, by blood
or marriage, to the ruling family. Clearly such a family was
bound to abuse its authority, and did. But its achievements were

T — D

considerable. It resettled nearly a million refugees from North Vietnam, distributed land to 140,000 landless peasants, restored rice production up to and beyond the pre-war level, and much else. But the régime was singularly out of touch with the Vietnamese people. Nhu's secret organizations told him who was likely to be plotting against him and his brothers in the Army or among the intellectuals, but not what the Communists were up to in the villages. Diem ruled from afar, and the family, though feared and obeyed, was hated.

For five or six years, however, Diem could do no wrong in American eyes. Disillusionment set in gradually from 1960. In November 1961 the censored Vietnamese press came out in a rash of anti-American headlines, arising out of reports that General Taylor had called on President Diem to liberalize his régime. During the spring and summer of 1963, the régime was involved in serious troubles with the Buddhist community, which accused the Catholic Diem family of showing undue favour to its co-religionaries. A good deal of nonsense was written about this crisis, partly through exaggerated accounts of the strength of Buddhist numbers and feeling in South Vietnam. Nevertheless the régime was deservedly given a bad press throughout the world, especially when Madame Nhu, referring to public suicides of Buddhist monks by self-immolation, described them as a 'barbecue'. American public opinion was deeply offended by this callousness, and relations between the two countries took a further turn for the worse. In September, the powerful American Secretary of Defence, Mr McNamara, accompanied General Taylor on a further visit to Vietnam and their joint report, on their return to Washington, in effect dissociated the U.S. from the Diem régime. This amounted to a reversal of the policy of unconditional support initiated in 1954. It was therefore hardly a surprise when a group of Vietnamese army officers, headed by the jovial General Duong Van Minh, overthrew Diem on 1 November. It was General Minh who had swept rebels out of Saigon in the spring of 1955 when they were besetting Diem from all sides.

Diem and Nhu were murdered by the 1963 revolutionaries. Can, the political boss of the centre, was brought to trial for extortion and murder, and executed on 9 May 1964. Thus four of the six Ngo brothers had died violent deaths. It was an ignominious end to America's search for a Vietnamese strong man. But the war went on, and the Americans were increasingly involved in it.

Though, on the whole, the American military effort had been unsuccessful, it had kept the Viet Cong on the move, so that they had been unable to set up 'liberated zones' and proclaim a government. One of Nhu's constructive initiatives had been to push on with the building of 'strategic hamlets', in effect fortified villages designed to isolate and protect the peasants. But many of these were infiltrated by the Viet Cong, whose recruitment rate, running at 6,000 a year, remained high. The problem was to cut down this recruitment rate – that is, reduce popular support for the Communists.

Minh, though popular, was ineffectual, and he was overthrown on 30 January 1964 by another junta, headed by General Nguyen Khanh. Unlike Minh, Khanh lacked popular support. This he tried to remedy by broadcasting his government and winning over the important politico-religious sects.* But General Khanh soon revealed a frightening incapacity to govern while directing the war effort. On 25 August he resigned in the face of Buddhist and student demonstrators; he later withdrew his resignation, but in ambiguous terms, and a period of political and administrative confusion set in, which the Viet Cong guerrillas turned to profit with ever bolder aggressions and outrages. The American dilemma, from mid-September on, was whether the territory of South Vietnam could be defended without a direct occupation by United States troops that would look uncomfortably like the colonialism they were pledged to oppose.

LAOS†

In Laos, too, the search for a strong man was, in the end, counter-productive. In common with Cambodia and Vietnam,

---

* See below: Part Four, Chapter 3.

† In this section I have concentrated on American policy in Laos. The story of Viet Minh infiltration, of the growth of the Pathet Lao, and of the international crisis, is told in Part Four, Chapter 2.

Laos had emerged from the Indo-China war at least nominally independent. But sovereignty did not make this roadless stretch of land viable. The French had kept it going as an idyllic backwater; now the Americans set about transforming it into an anti-Communist bulwark. In effect, they became paymasters to the army and civil service, at an annual cost of $50 million. The principal opponent of the American policy, at least in the eyes of the State Department, was Prince Souvanna Phouma, who wanted Laos to be neutral, who defined neutrality as the right to accept aid from both sides in the East–West struggle, and who thought of the country's Communist problem as a simple family quarrel between himself and his half-brother, Prince Souphannouvong, leader of the Pathet Lao movement. As we have seen, the Geneva agreements of 1954 had left the Pathet Lao in physical possession of two provinces of Laos. Broadly speaking, the Americans were in favour of military action to reassert the government's authority in the two provinces, while Souvanna Phouma wanted to negotiate with his half-brother, and integrate the Pathet Lao forces and 'civil service' into the Laotian army and administration. Souvanna Phouma got his way in November 1957, in an agreement under which Prince Souphannouvong formally transferred the two provinces to the king's authority while he and another Pathet Lao representative were given portfolios in Souvanna Phouma's government.

This was more than the Americans were prepared to stomach, and in 1958 they managed to get Souvanna Phouma sent to Paris as ambassador. Shortly afterwards, they thought they had found the strong man they were looking for, in the person of an expansive, French-trained (but anti-French) army officer, General Phoumi Nosavan. General Phoumi became the leading influence in an American-supported political alliance of army officers and civil servants, known as the Comité pour la Défense des Intérêts Nationaux (CDIN), which swept into power in general elections in April 1960.

At this stage, the success of the State Department's 'strong man' policy seemed complete. The 'red prince', Souphannouvong, and fourteen other Communist leaders, were under house arrest in Vientiane; and the anti-Communists seemed firmly in the saddle, with the neutralist Souvanna Phouma safely out of the way. The success of American policy was, however, very short-lived. In May, Souphannouvong and the other Communists escaped from detention in mysterious circumstances and joined the Pathet Lao forces in the jungle. In August, a young paratroop officer, Captain Kong Lae (American-trained, but anti-American), took over in Vientiane and swept the right-wingers out of office in a lightning *coup d'état*. Kong Lae was a neutralist, not a Communist, but he took the view that the United States was the principal obstacle to Laotian neutrality. Accordingly his 'revolutionary committee's' neutralist statements had a decidedly anti-American tinge.

The advent of Kong Lae made it possible for Souvanna Phouma to return. On 15 August, a week after the *coup d'état*, he formed a government committed to neutrality. Meanwhile, General Phoumi and his supporters set up headquarters at Savannakhet, in the south. The American Central Intelligence Agency had a mission in Laos, known as the Programme Evaluations Office, under the 'faceless' General Hentges and its 'military advisers', numbering a few hundred men trained in guerrilla tactics and attached to General Phoumi's forces, began to organize the general's return to power. In December, General Phoumi fought his way back into Vientiane and Prince Souvanna Phouma took refuge in Cambodia.

Again, however, success proved illusory. Driven out of Vientiane, General Kong Lae, as he became, formed a tactical alliance with the Pathet Lao. And now both the Russians and the North Vietnamese Communists intervened. While in power, Souvanna Phouma had opened diplomatic relations with the Soviet Union and the Russians had airlifted food and petrol to Vientiane when General Phoumi had cut supplies off. Now the Russians started flying in arms to the Kong Lae–Pathet Lao forces; and the Vietnamese Communists sent officers, men, and arms to reinforce the neutral–Communist alliance in the field. Within a few weeks, General Phoumi found that all he really controlled of Laos was Vientiane, Savannakhet, and their environs. The Communists controlled most of the rest.

About this time, in January 1961, President Kennedy came to

power. It soon became clear that the new administration was aware that its predecessor's Laotian policy was in ruins. Could something be saved from the wreckage? One way might have been by collective action, with the allies of the United States within SEATO. Another was by negotiations. The first possibility was put to the test at the end of March 1961, when SEATO's ministerial council met in Bangkok. The new American Secretary of State, Mr Dean Rusk, however, found his British and French colleagues unwilling to support collective action. The next thing was to negotiate.

This was the background to the fourteen-nation conference on Laos, which opened in Geneva on 16 May. As we have seen, in connexion with Chinese policies, the conference began in sterility and recriminations. In Laos, meanwhile, General Phoumi was trying to make good his earlier victory; but on 6 May 1962 – almost exactly a year after the Geneva conference had opened – his forces were routed by the Pathet Lao. Once again, the strong man had proved a disappointment.

THE ROLE OF SEATO

It is perhaps characteristic of SEATO that my first mention of it in this chapter should have been in connexion with a failure. And yet at the time of its creation, it had seemed to fill a need. Certainly drama was not lacking in the circumstances. Let us recall them.

We are back in the dying days of the first Indo-China war. Mr Dulles had failed to persuade his British and French allies to endorse his plan for a massive blow to relieve pressure on Dien Bien Phu. Then came the Geneva conference and the partition of Vietnam under agreements from which the United States dissociated itself. By any reckoning the West had suffered a major defeat, however successful Mendès-France and Anthony Eden had been in limiting the consequences of the Communist victory in Indo-China. Something had to be done, both to demonstrate that the West had not exhausted its resources in the Far East and to warn the Communist powers of the dangers of further encroachments on other people's territory.

To these ends, Mr Dulles went ahead with plans for collective defence in South-East Asia which had been under discussion for some time. The British were keen to bring the so-called Colombo Powers – India, Pakistan, Burma, Ceylon, and Indonesia – who were thus known because they had met in Colombo and Kandy in April and May, into any discussions on defence in the region. But Mr Nehru was against the whole idea. The phase of delusion in India's foreign policy was at its height. Mr Nehru placed absolute faith in the Five Principles incorporated in the Sino-Indian agreement on Tibet, and which we quoted in the last chapter. In June 1954, when Mr Chou En-lai visited Delhi, Mr Nehru had asked him for an assurance that China would not interfere in South-East Asia, and especially in Laos and Cambodia, which were of particular interest to India because of their cultural connexions with Hinduism. Chou was ready to give any reassurance the Indian Prime Minister wanted but on condition that the Western powers also subscribed to the Five Principles. But this the West obstinately (in Mr Nehru's view) refused to do, and his vision of an 'area of peace' was fading in the hard light of America's determination to organize collective defence in South-East Asia. In short, Mr Nehru was not prepared to discuss such plans with the Western powers; and neither were the Indonesians, Burmese, or Ceylonese. The only Colombo power that was willing was Pakistan, and this largely for anti-Indian reasons that had little to do with fear of Communist aggression.

Apart from Pakistan, the only Asian powers that were prepared to discuss collective defence arrangements were Siam (which did not share the prevalent anti-colonial preconceptions) and the Philippines, which remained on good terms with the United States. The pact that later emerged from Mr Dulles's apprehensions and labours was thus weakened at the outset by the inadequacy of its Asian element; and Mr Nehru, whose short-sightedness and wishful blindness brought retribution in the Himalayan fighting of 1962, must bear a major share of the responsibility for SEATO's bad start.

In the event, the conference Mr Dulles had been proposing met in Manila from 6–8 September 1954. Apart from the three

Asian countries mentioned above, the participants were the United States, Britain, France, Australia, and New Zealand. The treaty that emerged was styled the 'South-East Asia Collective Defence Treaty', but is often called the Manila Treaty or just SEATO, from the treaty organization that was later set up in Bangkok. The drafting of the text was a meticulous compound of vagueness and precision. The definition of the treaty area illustrates this duality; it was defined as

... the general area of South-East Asia, including also the entire territories of the Asian parties, and the general area of the South-West Pacific area north of 21 degrees 30 minutes north latitude.

What did this mean? If one looks at a map one sees that the precise reference to the South-West Pacific excluded Formosa: nobody was particularly anxious to be drawn into a war with the Chinese Communists in defence of Chiang Kai-shek. But was India part of the treaty area? Presumably not, although the text did not specifically exclude India. But Pakistan was, and Pakistan consists of two half-countries separated by 1,000 miles of Indian territory. There was thus a studied vagueness about the Western end of the treaty area. When the matter was put to the test with the Chinese attack on India in the autumn of 1962, SEATO was not seized of it.

The signatories agreed that should any of them be attacked each would 'act to meet the common danger in accordance with its constitutional processes'. This protective proviso was specifically extended to cover three non-signatories: South Vietnam, Cambodia, and Laos. And in case any signatory should ever nurse the notion of calling in SEATO in the event of a clash with a non-Communist neighbour (e.g. Pakistan versus India) the United States appended an 'understanding' that the treaty applied only to *Communist* aggression.

I thought at the time, and still think, that there was a case for SEATO in the context of the French military disaster in Indo-China. In effect, the treaty drew an imaginary line, admittedly vague in places, north of South-East Asia and warned the Communist powers not to follow up their Indo-China success with aggression beyond existing boundaries. It is true that the same purpose could have been achieved by a declaration by the United States – either alone or in conjunction with other Western powers – but it was thought, probably rightly, that a treaty with *some* Asian members was better than a purely Western initiative. True again, the treaty would have been much more effective if it had included even one other major Asian country. But Mr Dulles and his allies rightly thought that they had more to lose by appearing to let Mr Nehru dictate their policy than by going ahead with their defence plans as best they could.

Despite its ill-favoured birth, SEATO did, for some years, enjoy a modest success. From 1954 to 1961, there was no Communist aggression of consequence in the treaty area. Members of the treaty took pleasure in attributing this relative peace to SEATO's deterrent influence; though cynics could point out that the presence of the U.S. Seventh Fleet in the Far East and the readiness of the British air–naval base in Singapore would have been deterrents anyway, even if there had been no SEATO. Then again, there were other factors at work. For reasons we have discussed, China had embarked on a conciliatory phase of diplomacy, which was reaffirmed after Mr Chou En-lai had heard for himself at Bandung how important his fellow-Asians thought it was that Asia should be at peace. Another factor in the protracted calm was the developing nuclear stalemate. But such factors probably weighed rather little in the minds of SEATO's Asian members: the Pakistanis, Siamese, and Filipinos seemed to feel comforted and protected by their membership of the Manila Treaty.

Such complacencies were shattered in 1961. In Laos, the Pathet Lao forces, trained, supplied, and even officered by North Vietnam, had gained control over large areas. In South Vietnam, Communist insurgents, known as Viet Cong, were pressing their attacks against the Diem régime; again, arms and men were reaching the insurgents, across Laos, from North Vietnam. Since Laos and Vietnam were both designated in the Manila Treaty as countries entitled to SEATO's protection, this situation was clearly a test case for the treaty organization. As I have mentioned, SEATO's ministerial council met in Bangkok in March 1961 to consider the situation, with special reference to Laos, but with Vietnam very much in mind. The treaty member most closely concerned with this situation was, of course, Siam which, as the British Foreign Secretary, Lord Home (as he then was), said in his opening statement on 27 March, had 'a long and vulnerable frontier' with Laos. There were other reasons for Siam's concern. A cultural and ethnic reason: the Lao are members of the Thai linguistic group and the Siamese and Laotians speak variants of the same language. A historical reason: Laos was once part of Siam. A family reason: the late Marshal Sarit, Siam's dictator at the time of the 1961 crisis, was an uncle of sorts to General Phoumi Nosavan, the Laotian 'strong man'.

The Western allies were, however, deeply divided at the time about the best course to adopt in Laos. The French had long supported Prince Souvanna Phouma's brand of neutralism and continued to recognize his government even after it had been ousted by Phoumi in December 1960, whereas the United States recognized the right-wing government under Prince Boun Oum, in which Phoumi was the Defence Minister. The British also recognized the Boun Oum government, but had serious reservations about its policies and went along with the French a good deal of the way in supporting Souvanna Phouma. One thing was certain: neither France nor Britain was prepared to support collective action by SEATO to save the day in Laos. The Americans thus found themselves isolated (in the company, it is true, of the Siamese and Filipinos) in pressing for some kind of action under the treaty. And, in the event, nothing was done.

This failure naturally had a disillusioning effect in Siam. In a general sense, the Siamese started asking themselves whether alignment with the West was as profitable as they had supposed. More specifically, what worried the Siamese most was the apparent demonstration that the treaty became inoperative if one of its members (in this instance, France) disagreed with proposals supported by other members. Did this mean that if Siam itself was threatened with aggression, the treaty would offer no protection? Such doubts – and the accompanying whispers of neutralism in Bangkok – were partly, though not wholly, allayed a year later. The Siamese Foreign Minister, Mr Thanat Khoman, visited Washington in March 1962, and on the 6th a joint statement was issued in his name and that of Mr Dean Rusk, the Secretary of State. This made the point that the American obligation to rescue Siam in the event of Communist aggression did not depend upon the prior agreement of other treaty members since 'this treaty obligation is individual as well as collective'. Just two months later, on 6 May, General Phoumi's forces were routed in Laos. This time, the United States didn't even wait to ask SEATO's advice, but immediately dispatched Marine and Army combat forces to Siam. Within a few days, British, Australian, New Zealand, and Philippine units – small but tangible – had joined the Americans. This was a demonstration of another kind: that SEATO sometimes worked better if its official machinery was *not* set in motion.

If Siam was comforted – as it was – in the spring of 1962, the same is not true of Pakistan later that year, when China launched an armed aggression against India, and Britain and the United States rushed emergency military supplies to the Indians. This, too, was a demonstration of another kind: that a country did not have to belong to SEATO to get Western aid if attacked by a Communist power; which, in turn, depreciated the value of membership. More specifically, however, the Pakistanis were worried in case the Indians – once the Chinese danger had passed – should use the arms they were getting from Britain and the United States against Pakistan. No amount of Western reassurances could sway them. And President Ayub Khan, although he had not, at the time of writing, actually taken Pakistan out of SEATO, drew closer to China in various ways: for instance by signing agreements with the Chinese Communists on frontier, trade, and civil aviation matters. This was at once a form of reinsurance on Pakistan's part, and a warning to the West that the Pakistanis could not be taken for granted just because they belonged to SEATO and CENTO (the former Baghdad Pact).

On the whole, then, it is hard to present SEATO as a success story. True, it has done and continues to do useful work in cultural and economic matters and in exchanging information on security. But these are marginal things. In the major matter of defending the treaty area against Communist aggression SEATO has conspicuously failed to do what it was supposed to do.

This severe verdict has seemed, if anything, even truer after more recent SEATO Ministerial Council Meetings. France boycotted the meetings at Canberra, in June 1966, and in Washington, in April 1967. At the Canberra meeting, Britain dissociated itself from the bombing of Hanoi by the Americans; Pakistan urged a compromise over Vietnam; and the more active Asian members, Siam and the Philippines, had harsh words about members which did not pull their weight. At the Washington meeting, the British stuck to their role as potential peacemakers – a curiously uncommitted one for members of a military alliance, and heard themselves attacked by the Australians for pulling forces out of the Far East because Indonesia had ended its confrontation with Malaysia. The Pakistanis went further than the British by publicly dissociating themselves from the communiqué.

In effect, then, three of the original members of the alliance – Britain, France and Pakistan – had dropped out. But the escalation of the war in Vietnam and the growing threat to Siam did at least cement the bond between the active members.

Part Four TROUBLE-SPOTS

Chapter One

NEO-IMPERIALISM: INDO-CHINA
AND INDONESIA

We have had 'neo-colonialism', 'revisionism', and 'poly-centrism', among others, and I now offer yet another neologism: 'neo-imperialism'. Frankly, I should prefer to call it 'the new imperialism'; but Professor Hugh Seton-Watson, Robert Conquest, and others have used this term to refer to Soviet imperialism conducted in the name of 'anti-imperialism'. Such is the semantic confusion of our times.

By 'neo-imperialism', then, I mean the attempts being made by the governments of former colonies to create empires of their own in the wake of the departing Westerners. There is no dearth of examples in the contemporary world, but two are of direct bearing on the turmoil of South-East Asia today: the neo-imperialisms of Indonesia and North Vietnam. Imperialism has many definitions, including Lenin's irrelevant one which related it to capitalism (there were empires before capitalism was heard of). But the most generally acceptable one is that it is a territorial extension of nationalism at the expense of weaker nations. The neo-imperialisms of North Vietnam and Indonesia both come within this definition.

Both indeed have long historical roots. Essentially the imperialism of Ho Chi Minh is a revival of traditional Vietnamese encroachments on neighbouring territories, the more implacable for being conducted in the name of a totalitarian creed. To some extent, of course, Indonesia's imperialism must be referred to in the past tense, since it was inspired and directed by President Sukarno who has now been stripped of his power to do mischief. But Sukarno's dream of empire, though faded, cannot simply be dismissed as dead history. For years, he led the great mass of the Indonesian people in a mounting spiral of self-deluding exaltation, matched at home by a descending spiral of corruption and bankruptcy. The traces of his misrule and irredentist folly live on; and one cannot rule out the possibility that some future and abler demagogue may try to succeed where he failed in his imperialist ambitions. The story of his dream of empire must therefore be retold here.

Sukarno's imperialism was quite simply an attempt to reconstitute the Javanese empire of Madjapahit, which was at its height in the fourteenth century. It may be difficult to grasp such concepts; indeed it is generally conceded that it is difficult to see the wood if one focuses too sharply on the trees. In these instances, the 'trees' are the forest of semantic pitfalls with which the path of the explorer is strewn. We have been so accustomed to hearing Sukarno (and Ho Chi Minh) shout against imperialism and about liberating people from neo-colonialism (or plain colonialism) that we may have found it hard to see that what in fact they were doing was to extend their own dominion over peoples who want none of it. Similarly, as Madame Roland remarked on the way to the scaffold, what crimes were committed in the name of liberty! There is another mental blockage to be disposed of: the notion that Communism and nationalism are irreconcilables. It is true enough that nationalism is often an obstacle to the spread of Communism; but Communism is sometimes harnessed to the service of nationalism. This is as true of Ho Chi Minh as it is of Mao Tse-tung.

Since it is unfashionable for intending conquerors to trumpet their intentions, one has to catch them unawares. This simply means going far enough back in one's researches. In President Sukarno's case, for instance, the things he did and said in 1945 are more helpful (that is, revealing) than those he said in his series of speeches threatening to 'crush' Malaysia. In an earlier chapter on collaboration and resistance (see p. 40)

I recalled the fact that Sukarno was present at a meeting of Malays shortly before Japan's defeat in 1945, at which a Japanese-sponsored plan to create a Greater Indonesia, to include the Malay peninsula, was discussed. In Java itself, on 1 March, the Japanese military administrator had set up an Investigating Committee for the Preparation of Indonesia's Independence (*Badan Penjelidek Usaha Persiapan Kemerdekaan Indonesia*) whose proceedings are possibly of even greater interest now than they were at the time. On 11 July, the committee voted in favour of a motion declaring that Malaya and British Borneo should form part of an independent Indonesia.

Sukarno was among those who voted in favour; and this alone helps to explain the poison of frustration that so clearly tormented him before the spectacle of independent Malaysia. His speech before the Indonesian independence committee in July 1945, however, showed that his deeper ambitions stretch well beyond the confines of Indonesia plus Malaya. He began significantly by declaring that he was not an imperialist, but added that he had never said Indonesia comprised only areas that had been ruled by the Dutch. 'In fact,' he said, 'I have on one occasion in my life dreamt of a Pan-Indonesia, which will include not only Malaya and Papua (New Guinea) but also the Philippines.' But he thought, with evident reluctance, that there need be no more talk of Pan-Indonesia because 'the Philippines is already independent, and we must respect the sovereignty of the Philippine nation'.

In another significant passage, Sukarno made a reference to the Kingdom of Madjapahit and went on to a peroration that is worth quoting for the light it throws on his dreams of grandeur:

God has determined that certain parts of the world should form single units – the British Isles as one, and likewise the Hellenic islands, and India surrounded by the ocean below and the Himalayas above. God has also determined on the map which He has created that the Japanese isles should form one single unit. *And when I look at the islands situated between Asia and Australia and between the Pacific and the Indian Oceans, I understand that they are meant to form a single entity.* (My italics.)

If we in turn follow Sukarno's advice and look at God's map,

we shall find that the area described in the passage I have itali-
cized includes the Philippines as well as the islands that form
part of the present Republic of Indonesia. The term 'between
Asia and Australia', on the other hand, suggests the exclusion
of Malaya, but the inclusion of the whole of the island of New
Guinea, the eastern half of which is Australian-administered.
However, Sukarno went on to clarify his views by saying he
advocated the inclusion of 'Malaya and Papua' in independent
Indonesia, though again without specifying what he meant by
Papua. An earlier speaker had defined Papua as 'that part (of
New Guinea) which used to be ruled by the Dutch'.

Sukarno's speech was as clear a statement of neo-imperialist
ambitions as we are ever likely to hear from the mouth of a
politician disclaiming imperialist intentions. It is only fair to
add that at the same meeting in July 1945, an honest and
moderate statesman, Dr Mohammed Hatta, who later became
Indonesia's Vice-President, sagely argued in favour of an independent Malaya and of the right of the Papuans to independence. Dr Hatta's words, too, are worth quoting, for they are a
reminder that there are sensible and honourable Indonesian
politicians as well as the other kind.

Referring to the theory, expressed the previous day by another speaker, that Malaya and Papua should be included in
Indonesia on strategic grounds, Dr Hatta commented:

Chamberlain (*sic*) might say that the boundary of England
does not extend to the English Channel only but as far as the
Rhine. If this sort of thing is proceeded with, it is possible that
we shall not be satisfied with Papua only and that we may want
to include the Solomons and so on as far as the middle of the
Pacific Ocean. Can we possibly defend such a large territory?
Have we got the capacity to administer the whole territory of
our motherland including these new ones?

Dr Hatta also rejected another speaker's argument that the
Papuans were of the same race as the Indonesians.

But such views were too sensible to carry weight in an assembly dominated by Sukarno. In later years Dr Hatta found it an
increasingly frustrating experience to be Vice-President under

Sukarno. In 1956 he could stand it no longer and resigned.

Ho Chi Minh has not, as far as I am aware, favoured us with as clear a statement of imperialist aims as Sukarno, but the evidence is strong enough. As we saw in Part Two, Chapter 1, he had founded the Indo-China Communist Party in 1930. At first, in March that year, the party was called the Vietnam Cong San Dang or Vietnam Communist Party; but in October, the name was changed to Dong Duong Cong San Dang (Indo-China Communist Party) with the declared purpose of serving the entire territory of what was then French Indo-China, which included Cambodia and Laos as well as Vietnam. Ever since, Ho has pursued the unwavering objective of uniting all three countries under Vietnamese Communist rule. This has remained true through the many changes of outward clothing made by the Vietnamese Communists. One of these we saw in Part Two, Chapter 3: the Communists formed the Viet Minh front with other parties in 1941. Four years later, in November 1945, the mystification was completed when the Indo-China Communist Party 'dissolved' itself. This was shortly after the proclamation of Ho Chi Minh's Democratic Republic of Vietnam, and the dissolution of the CP had two objects: to show that the Vietnamese Communists no longer had designs on Laos and Cambodia and to give Vietnamese nationalists the impression that Ho and the other Communist leaders had opted out of the international Communist movement. The Communist Party kept its organization intact, however, and the party re-emerged in February 1951 under the name of Vietnam Workers' Party (Vietnam Lao Dong Dang). Here again there was a coyness about the title, which avoided using the term 'Communist'; and the party was called Vietnamese, not Indo-Chinese. But this did not mean that it had lost interest in the other countries of Indo-China, for the 'National Congress' that had been convened to launch the new party specifically called for increased assistance to the 'resistance movements' in those two countries. By this time, of course, the first Indo-China war had been in progress for more than four years.

The innocent-sounding formula of aid to resistance movements was another disguise. It was intended to conceal the fact that the Vietnamese Communists planned to coordinate these groups under their own direction. To this end they selected two willing tools. In Laos: Prince Souphannouvong. In Cambodia: a Vietnamese-Cambodian Communist called Sieu Heng. Let us see what these men did.

The Cambodian Communists never managed to set up an anti-French resistance movement. The Communist guerrillas that were active in Cambodia during the last two years of the first Indo-China war numbered only a few hundreds and consisted entirely of Viet Minh irregulars (see Part Two, Chapter 3). The considerably larger Khmer Issarak movement was non-Communist, though towards the end it kept in touch with the Viet Minh groups. In the face of these facts, Sieu Heng, Hanoi's agent, styled himself the chief of a 'Cambodian Liberation Army' which existed only on paper. But Sieu Heng had other, only slightly more real, functions. He was the chairman of a body called 'Central Office South', another creation of the Vietnamese Communists, which had given it 'authority' over south and south-central Vietnam *and over Cambodia*. At first, Sieu Heng's 'office' was based in South Vietnam; later he moved headquarters to south-west Cambodia, a trackless semi-wilderness well endowed for concealment. From there, he established contact with the Viet Minh groups operating in Cambodia, and with the Khmer Issaraks. Just possibly, Sieu Heng could have been the mysterious 'Son Ngoc Minh', an apparently mythical Cambodian 'resistance leader' whose claims were canvassed by the Communist delegations at the Geneva conference in 1954. But there is no evidence to support this theory.

Indeed Sieu Heng can be positively identified only in one other connexion. The Lao Dong congress in February 1951 had been followed by a major act of Vietnamese Communist policy. In March the party called delegates from the so-called People's United Fronts of Cambodia and Laos to a joint conference. These bodies were offshoots of the Vietnam People's United Front, known as the Lien Viet from two of the components of its name in Vietnamese (Hoi *Lien*-Hiep Quoc-Dan *Viet*nam), formed in May 1946 by Ho Chi Minh to bring all sectors of the Vietnamese population under the authority of the theoretically dissolved Communist Party. The three United Fronts (including the Lien Viet) set up a Joint National United Front for the whole of Indo-China. The short-term aim of the new Indo-China United Front was to provide cover and justification for the use of Cambodian and Laotian territory by the Viet Minh in its war with the French. The long-term aim was to provide an extension of Vietnamese Communist rule over Cambodia and Laos. The Vietnamese clearly wanted to invest the occasion with historic significance for the inaugural conference issued a manifesto 'urging the peoples of the world to support the joint national united front'. The Cambodian and Laotian 'delegates', however, represented nobody but themselves. The Cambodian was Sieu Heng, who had no mandate whatever from the Khmer people. The Laotian was that princely dissident Souphannou-vong.

I have already mentioned (in Part Two, Chapter 3) Souph-annouvong's membership of the short-lived anti-French Lao Issara government in September 1945. This curious figure, intellectually brilliant but with a gift for bitterness, had brought nothing but harm to his country. Born in 1912 and a graduate of the School of Civil Engineering in Paris, he developed a deep resentment on discovering that he was drawing less money than his French colleagues, when, on returning to Indo-China, he found a job with the Trans-Indo-Chinese Railway. This is a fairly typical experience of colonial days. In Souphannouvong's case it seems to have turned him into a professional rebel for life. The Lao Issara government was soon driven into exile in Siam and Prince Souphannouvong, as its 'Foreign Minister', became the leading advocate of armed insurrection. He was in touch with the Viet Minh and proposed that the Lao Issara movement should merge with that Vietnamese front. In 1947 he married the daughter of a Vietnamese postal employee, and this was a decisive event in his life, for his wife, though she has kept in the background, is a confirmed Marxist. In the spring of 1949, Souphannouvong's brothers and other colleagues tired of his talk of an alliance with the Vietnamese and expelled him from the Lao Issara. This was 1 May. Some months later, Souphannouvong, together with a few Lao Issara rebels, left Bangkok to join the Viet Minh in Tonking. From there he was sent to China for a Communist indoctrination course. He has continued to work closely with the Viet Minh ever since.

In the light of this record, it is odd that Souphannouvong has always strenuously maintained that he is no Communist. In 1962, turning up in Geneva during the international conference on Laos, he angrily denied charges of Communist affiliations. In this his neutralist half-brother, Prince Souvanna Phouma, stoutly supported him. On 1 April 1961, for instance, I had one of a number of conversations with Souvanna Phouma (in a London hotel), and he impatiently dismissed my suggestion that Souphannouvong was a Communist. 'Souphannouvong is a patriot,' he said. 'I don't know about his wife: I haven't asked her for her opinions.'

Such talk, however, should not fool anybody. Whether or not Souphannouvong is technically a Communist, he has consistently acted as the willing instrument of Vietnamese Communist neo-imperialism.

*

Ho Chi Minh's neo-imperialist ambitions have not stopped at Laos. He was active in Siam during the 1920s (see p. 38) and his Communist Party, through all its changes of name, has kept close links with the Siamese Communists. An obvious channel for subversion has been the 40,000 left-wing Vietnamese living in Siam's north-eastern provinces, who took refuge there in the 1930s. As we have seen (p. 87), North Vietnam as well as China is involved in the Communist terrorism which started in these provinces in 1965. Siamese Communist defectors admitted in March 1967 that they had received ideological training in Laos and North Vietnam, in particular at a Thai Communist Party political and military school allowed to function in Hoa Binh (North Vietnam). In consequence, the Thai Patriotic Front, whose 1,700 to 2,000 guerrillas now operate in groups of 100 to 200, is coming more and more to resemble the National Front for the Liberation of South Vietnam, in structure and technique.

VIET MINH INFILTRATION

Northern Laos is a region of towering, hump-backed mountains, deep valleys, and rain-forest. The frontier dividing it from North Vietnam is vague and the Thai tribes straddling the border look the same and speak the same on either side of it. There is no more perfect terrain in the world for tactics of quiet infiltration. The Vietnamese Communists have made full use of these opportunities, slipping across the border at will, and back again if anybody – such as the International Control Commissions set up after each of the Geneva conferences – showed signs of looking too closely.

In their imperialist encroachments on Laos, the Vietnamese Communists have sometimes done the invading themselves and sometimes left it to Souphannouvong and his followers, but always with a tight control over events. Before going to North Vietnam, Souphannouvong had formed a Lao Liberation Committee. In August 1950 this body convened a conference of Laotian exiles in North Vietnam. Calling themselves the Laotian National Assembly, the exiles proclaimed a Laotian United Front and a Liberation government of the Pathet Lao (Lao State), with Souphannouvong as 'Prime Minister'. The Pathet Lao was to have its own 'People's Liberation Army'.

As we saw in the preceding chapter, the Laotian United Front was later merged with the Cambodian Front and the Lien Viet into a Front covering the whole of Indo-China. Two pieces of documentary evidence show that the Vietnamese Communists intended to gain and keep the direction of the 'liberation' movement in Cambodia and Laos as well as Vietnam. One of these is a captured Viet Minh document, dated November 1951 and intended for the guidance of the party men who controlled the Viet Minh Front. The relevant passage read:

... the creation of a separate party for each of the three nations does not prejudice the revolutionary movement in Indo-China. ... The Vietnamese Party reserves the right to supervise the activities of its brother parties in Cambodia and Laos.

The other piece of evidence is a Viet Minh broadcast which – like the document I have just quoted – was probably not intended for the eyes and ears of the outside world. It was quoted by Reuter on 13 April 1953, and included a message from a Viet Minh 'delegation to Cambodia', which ran:

The Lao Dong Party and the people of Vietnam have the mission to make revolution in Cambodia and Laos. We, the Viet Minh elements, have been sent to serve this revolution and to build the union of Vietnam, Cambodia, and Laos.

That very month – April 1953 – several battalions of the Viet Minh regular army, thinly disguised as 'people's volunteers' on the model offered by the Chinese Communist army in Korea, invaded Laos. In theory the Viet Minh 'volunteers' were helping Souphannouvong's 'liberation army'. In fact it was the Viet Minh that did all the fighting. They rapidly overran Sam Neua province and drew near Luang Prabang, the royal capital. Comforted by Buddhist soothsayers, the aged King Sisavang Vong refused to leave his palace. French Union reinforcements halted the Viet Minh, but although the 'volunteers' withdrew, they left a political time-bomb behind: Souphannouvong. The 'red prince' had moved headquarters to the town of Sam Neua, the provincial capital, and there, on 19 April, he proclaimed the Pathet Lao and asserted that its government was the only lawful authority in Laos. Neither the Soviet Union nor the Chinese People's Republic, however, bothered to recognize it.

The Viet Minh army invaded Laos twice again during the first Indo-China war: in December 1953 and in February 1954. Three months later (as we saw in Part Three, Chapter 1), during the Geneva conference, the Vietnamese Communists were pressing for the recognition of the Pathet Lao as an independent negotiating partner; but even the Chinese Communists didn't support this pretence.

Nevertheless, the Pathet Lao emerged from the conference in a powerful position to make mischief – not through diplomatic channels, but where it mattered: on the ground in Sam Neua and Phong Saly provinces, in which Souphannouvong was in *de facto* control.

This was indeed the decisive fact. On paper, the Geneva agreements, to which the Vietnamese Communists were a party, had recognized the sovereignty of the Royal Laotian government over the whole of Laos, including the two Communist-controlled provinces. It had been agreed that the Pathet Lao movement would be 're-integrated' within the national community; but, 'pending a settlement', the 'fighting units of "Pathet Lao"' were to be concentrated in Sam Neua and Phong Saly.

This sounded encouraging. But it took more than three years to reach a 'settlement'; and thereafter, no mutually acceptable definition of 're-integration' was ever drafted.

From the Royal government's point of view, these were infinitely frustrating years. From the Communist point of view, they were time well spent. The Viet Minh had created the Pathet Lao movement in some haste but the war had prevented it from giving full attention to its political indoctrination. With the Geneva settlement came the chance to remedy this shortcoming. A good deal is known of Viet Minh methods during this period through the detailed statements of Pathet Lao defectors. The most informative was Major Kavinh Koenakorn, former secretary of the Pathet Lao political delegation in Vientiane, who was granted political asylum by the Royal government in September 1955.

At all levels, said the Major, Viet Minh control of the Pathet Lao was absolute. When the fighting was over, the Viet Minh had taken many women and children of Pathet Lao families to North Vietnam. This served a dual purpose: the Viet Minh now had both hostages and potential recruits. Many of those taken away were brought back later; they then resumed in Sam Neua the indoctrination courses that had begun in Hanoi. But each family of Pathet Lao men was expected to have one child or more educated in a Communist capital. In those days, there was no polycentrism, so it didn't matter which capital: Souphannou-vong, for instance, had two sons at school in Moscow.

Other Pathet Lao defectors confirmed Major Kavinh's evidence. One of them had this to say in an interview with Agence Lao-Presse on 26 November 1955:

I thought I was fighting in and for my own country, but the discipline imposed by the Viet Minh kept us in constant danger of deportation. The least argument, the smallest mistake, was greeted by the fatal words: 'to be sent to the instruction centre'. These instruction centres were in Vietnam, and no one who went there ever came back.

The Vietnamese Communists were aware that it would be difficult to get the Laotians to accept the Pathet Lao as a 'national liberation movement' if their own control was too visible. Their difficulty was that their raw material – the Laotians – were more easy-going than the Vietnamese, less readily fanatical and more likely to revert to comforting ancestral ways if the grip of the Viet Minh was relaxed. To overcome this difficulty, they resorted to all manner of subterfuges. Viet Minh agents in Sam Neua and Phong Saly were directed to assume Laotian names; more Lao Dong party members from the Thai minority areas of North Vietnam were sent across, as these could more readily merge with the population of the occupied provinces.

In microcosm, the Viet Minh occupation gave the people of north-eastern Laos a taste of the methods in use wherever a Communist party has gained control. Indoctrination courses for Pathet Lao recruits and compulsory political lectures for the population were put in train from the start. Landlords and 'counter-revolutionaries' were denounced and removed or otherwise eliminated. The purposes of the Lao Dong were clear enough: potential enemies had to be put out of the way; a solidly indoctrinated Pathet Lao organization had to be created, competent to do the Viet Minh's work, if necessary without Vietnamese Communists at its side; and finally, a clandestine network had to be established *before* a settlement was reached with the Royal government, so that the work of subversion could continue thereafter.

To this end, Pathet Lao agents were sent to villages throughout Laos. There, cells were set up and anti-government propaganda was distributed. Likely-looking villagers were enrolled in jungle schools for indoctrination. Arms were hidden, together with stocks of clothing and food – all this against the day of a settlement, so that, at a signal from Hanoi, guerrilla war could begin. As a matter of fact, throughout this lengthy period of preparation, which coincided for part of the time with protracted negotiations between the Pathet Lao and the government, fighting of varying intensity did go on, mostly on the perimeter of the occupied provinces. The government knew or suspected what the Viet Minh were up to. Growing impatient with the delay, it sought to assert its undoubted sovereignty over the two provinces, and in so doing clashed with the Viet Minh officered Pathet Lao guerrillas. On the Pathet Lao side, heavily backed by Hanoi's propaganda machine, much stress was laid on the proviso that the Pathet Lao men could be concentrated in the two provinces 'pending a political settlement' (Article 14 of the Laotian cease-fire agreement). So long as a political settlement could be deferred, the Communists could argue, however speciously, that they were within their rights. And so the negotiations dragged on, sometimes in Vientiane, sometimes in Rangoon, with Souphannouvong referring every issue to Hanoi for instructions and gaining more time for the Pathet Lao to organize itself.

THE PATHET LAO IN THE OPEN

Though the Vietnamese Communist presence in Laos has ebbed and flowed according to expediency and tactical needs,

Hanoi has maintained its iron grip on the Pathet Lao movement. By the time Souphannouvong had reached agreement with the Royal Laotian government, the groundwork for continued subversion had been pretty thoroughly laid. This was in November 1957. On the 18th, Souphannouvong had formally transferred to the king of Laos the 'two provinces of Phong Saly and Sam Neua together with their administration and all the troops, civil servants, and military equipment of the fighting units of the Pathet Lao'. On the 19th, Souphannouvong's half-brother, Prince Souvanna Phouma, brought two Pathet Lao men into his cabinet. One was Souphannouvong, who became Minister of Planning, Reconstruction, and Urbanism; the other was a 'hard core' Communist, Phoumi Vongvichit, who was given the quaint portfolio of Religious Cults and the Fine Arts. To Prince Souvanna Phouma, who had always argued that the Pathet Lao trouble was just a family quarrel between him and his younger brother, this was to be the end of the road. Now, he thought, the political problem had been solved. It was, in fact, the beginning of an even stonier path than the Laotians had yet travelled, leading to further violence in a setting of chaos.

The agreement indeed became an instrument for the furtherance of Hanoi's aims. The Pathet Lao movement was now allowed to set up its own party, the Neo Lao Hak Sat (NLHS), which in May 1958 won nine seats in the National Assembly. On the surface, the NLHS was as respectable as any bourgeois political party. Indeed its members, though they had attended courses in Marxism–Leninism, were mostly not dedicated Communists, and indeed were under instructions not to bring Communist arguments too audibly into their speeches. The NLHS, however, was just a respectable front for a secret Communist body (*Phak Khon Ngan* or Worker's Party, named after the Vietnamese Lao Dong, which controlled it). Much smaller and more compact than the NLHS, the Phak Khon Ngan is organized in cells consisting entirely of hard-core Communists. New recruits have to swear unquestioning obedience to hierarchical superiors, regardless of the race of those giving the orders. Most of the key members of the Phak Khon Ngan also belong to the Vietnamese Lao Dong. A conspicuous exception is Prince Souphannouvong, who is useful to the Vietnamese Communists because of his name and personality, but who might have ambitions of his own and is therefore in the last resort expendable. Flattery and an expense allowance are available to him, but he is often excluded from policy decisions. There has been much argument about who the real leaders of the NLHS are (meaning the convinced executants of Hanoi's will). Phoumi Vongvichit, who served in Souvanna Phouma's 1957 government and is the NLHS's Secretary-General, is certainly one; Kaysone Phomivan is another. Both are members of the Vietnamese Lao Dong.

The chain of command thus extended from the Lao Dong, through the Phak Khon Ngan to the Neo Lao Hak Sat. After the 1957 agreement, the NLHS set up branches in many parts of Laos, including isolated villages, and duplicated the overt party offices with clandestine cells. Another way Hanoi wove its spider-web was through the 're-integration' of the Pathet Lao civil service and army. As the Pathet Lao people were sent back to their villages or to jobs in the country's few towns, they constituted so many indirect agents of the Lao Dong.

The whole business of 're-integration' was open to an infinitude of abuses. In 1954, there were only about 1,000 men in the Pathet Lao forces. By February 1958 there were 6,000. But on 18 February, when 1,500 of them were integrated into the Royal army, in a special ceremony in the Plain of Jars, only 2,500 rifles were handed in. As for the 1,500 (two battalions), an interminable argument soon developed over what 'integration' really meant. The Royal government argued that it meant dispersing the 1,500 throughout the army; the NLHS countered with the view that the two battalions, retaining their identity and cohesion, should simply be added to the existing army. There was also an argument over officers. The government said the Pathet Lao were entitled to the usual complement of officers for two battalions: forty-one. The Pathet Lao asked for 112 – enough for six battalions. In March 1959 – more than a year after the Plain of Jars ceremony – the government accepted this demand, but the Pathet Lao then raised fresh difficulties about back pay and the choice of officers. On 14 May the government, tiring of this prevarication, called on the Pathet Lao soldiers to choose between submitting, resigning from the army, or being declared rebels. One of the battalions gave in, but the other broke out of camp and made its way to the North Vietnam border.

This was the start of one of the most curious episodes of the long Laotian crisis. Soon Hanoi radio was claiming that the local population was 'rallying to the support of the Pathet Lao resistance forces', meaning the missing battalion. There is no evidence that this is what was happening. But by July the Royal army, in pursuit of the battalion, found it was up against much tougher resistance than a mere 700 or 800 retreating men could have put up. On the 29th, a Laotian communiqué mentioned attacks on army frontier posts and commented: 'It seems established that the rebel bands operating in the Sam Neua sector do not belong to the rebel battalion from the Plain of Jars but represent new elements entirely armed, equipped, and officered by the Democratic Republic of Vietnam.' This seems to have been the true meaning of Hanoi's vision of local people flocking to the Pathet Lao banner; if any flocking was done it was by recruits who must have been under training in North Vietnam for some time.

Though this was the reality, Western public opinion came to swallow a quite different version of the facts. On 4 August, the Laotian government proclaimed a state of emergency in five provinces and drew the attention of the Secretary-General of the United Nations, the late Mr Hammarskjöld, to North Vietnam's part in the threat to Laos. Exactly a month later, the Laotian government appealed for U.N. assistance. The Security Council met on 7 September and appointed a sub-committee to report on the facts. The sub-committee visited Laos between 15 September and 13 October and issued its report on 4 November.

Whether intentionally or not, most of the U.N. correspondents contrived to give the impression that the sub-committee had exonerated North Vietnam from the Laotian charges of aggression. This they did by concentrating on the last sentence but one of the sub-committee's report, which said: 'The ensemble of information submitted to the sub-committee did not clearly establish whether there were crossings of the frontier by regular troops of the DRVN' – Democratic Republic of (North) Vietnam.

Now these are neutral and cautious words, typical of the non-committal approach of a typical U.N. sub-committee. They could indeed be interpreted as saying that North Vietnamese aggression in Laos had not been proved. Or equally, as saying that North Vietnamese aggression had not been *dis*proved either. In London, leader writers faced with stories and head-lines suggesting that the whole thing had been cooked up by the Laotian government wrote their comments accordingly. And the public was left with the general impression that the men in Vientiane were simply crying 'Wolf!' for no good reason.

As a matter of fact, Vientiane communiqués had never been especially notable for their accuracy (in which the Laotian government is by no means alone); and within the next two or three years they became wilder still. But the balance of prob-ability, in the light of the background of Vietnamese Communist intervention I have outlined, strongly supports the contention that something much bigger than a spontaneous upsurge of local guerrillas was afoot in Laos that summer. For one thing, the guerrillas had all been either disarmed or included in the Royal army – with the one exception of the defecting battalion. Yet there had been fighting of some intensity in various places (of that the U.N. report left no doubt); where, then, did the forces hostile to the Laotian government come from ? But there are other observations to make. Only the naïve or the credulous could suppose that the Vietnamese Communists, assuming they had crossed the border, would wait around to give the U.N. sub-committee proof of their presence; or if they did wait around, that they would emerge from the jungle and show themselves to the visitors. Then again, the sub-committee's report, when it turned up, painted quite a different picture from the one sketched in by the U.N. reporters.

For instance the report pointed out (paragraphs 26 and 27) that the guerrilla areas were 'rugged with mountains' and 'covered by dense jungles, impenetrable except in certain places'; it was therefore not surprising that reports should be incomplete or contradictory. Moreover, Laotian witnesses had pointed out that government control was slack along the border, which could be crossed without restraint at certain points (paragraph 34). The report recorded details of border crossings from North Vietnam and the fact that the Vietnamese had been identified by 'the colour of their uniforms, the use of Roman script (as in Vietnam), the language spoken, and also by their staple food (common rice instead of glutinous rice, characteristic both of the Lao and of the Black and Red Thais from Laos)' (paragraph 64). Witnesses described how they had been captured by Pathet Lao forces and handed over to the Viet Minh; and peasants in battle areas said they had recognized Viet Minh soldiers from their uniforms and language. Finally, in its summary, the sub-committee recorded the view of forty of the forty-one witnesses questioned that 'the hostile elements received support from the territory of the DRVN, consisting mainly of equipment, arms, ammunition, supplies, and the help of political cadres'. In the light of this evidence, the lack of proof that *regular* North Vietnamese troops had crossed the border takes on a minor significance. There is no doubt at all that the whole episode is another chapter in the story of North Vietnamese neo-imperialism.

INTERNATIONAL CRISIS

There is no need to go over ground already covered in our chapter on SEATO and American intervention. But we must deal with the 1962 Laotian 'settlement' and its consequences.

When the delegates of fourteen nations reached agreement on the future of Laos at Geneva on 23 July 1962, they had been in session, on and off, for more than fourteen months. There had been innumerable wrangles. One had concerned the Laotian delegation. At first there were three delegations, representing (*a*) Prince Boun Oum's right-wing government, (*b*) Prince Souvanna Phouma's neutralist government, and (*c*) the Pathet Lao. As we saw in an earlier chapter, Boun Oum had been an ally of the French in 1945; now he was the darling of the Americans. Souvanna Phouma, violently anti-French in 1945, now found much support in France. General Phoumi, who had been the American-backed 'strong man', was now in trouble with the Americans for opposing the formation of a coalition government with Communist participation. King Savang Vatthana of Laos, remembering the part Souvanna Phouma had played in 'deposing' his father in 1945 (and 'abrogating' his own succession rights)* would have nothing to do with Souvanna Phouma's efforts to form a coalition. Exasperated, the Americans suspended economic aid to Boun Oum's government, which was virtually their creation. It was all maddeningly Laotian and normal.

In the end, the three tendencies in Laotian politics – as it became fashionable to call them – did form a 'government of national union', on 23 June 1962. Souvanna Phouma was Prime Minister and Minister of Defence; the Communist leader, Souphannouvong, became Vice-Premier in charge of economic planning; and the anti-Communist General Phoumi was the other Vice-Premier, in charge of finance. This was a piquant situation: in effect, Phoumi held the purse strings for the planning Souphannouvong hoped to carry out. It was also a political nonsense.

Everything had been held up at Geneva while the Communists, anti-Communists, and neutrals squabbled over jobs. Now they had settled their differences, at least on paper, it took the delegates only another month to complete their draft agreement, which came in two parts: a declaration on the neutrality of Laos and a protocol recording various undertakings by interested powers. Laos renounced military alliances and declared that it would

not allow the establishment of any foreign military base on Laotian territory, nor allow any country to use Laotian territory for military purposes or for the purposes of interference in the internal affairs of other countries, nor recognize the protection of any alliance or military coalition, including SEATO.

This was, in effect, a funeral oration for SEATO. The key phrase, however, was the one about not allowing any country to

* See Part Two, Chapter 3.

use Laos for military or interventionist purposes. The chief culprit throughout the Laotian events had been North Vietnam, though the declaration did not say so. In fact, with an aplomb that is astonishing in the face of the evidence, the North Vietnamese delegation at the conference went on to the last calmly denying that it had, or ever had had, troops in Laos. Whenever the Chinese and North Vietnamese delegates raised the question of evacuating foreign troops, they always added that they were referring to Americans, French, Siamese, South Vietnamese, and 'Chiang Kai-shek remnants' (a reference to Nationalist stragglers who had stayed in the region since the end of the Second World War). This exasperated even the patient and equable British co-chairman of the conference, Mr Malcolm MacDonald, who at one stage exclaimed:

> We all know that there are military advisers, military technicians from the Democratic Republic of Vietnam in Laos . . . and therefore we are entitled to get a straight answer from the representatives of the Democratic Republic of Vietnam.

But a straight answer was never to be had, though towards the end the Russians (but only the Russians and only in private) started admitting that there might be a few North Vietnamese in Laos. This hypocrisy made nonsense of the guarantees written into the protocol, in particular the provision that 'all foreign regular and irregular troops, foreign para-military formations and foreign military personnel' were to be withdrawn from Laos within a stated time. On 7 October, the United States was able to announce that all its men had left.

There had been 800 American 'advisers' in Laos at the height of the crisis. Their withdrawal, which had been verified by the International Control Commission, was a considerable act of faith on Washington's part, the more so as only three dozen or so North Vietnamese had checked out. At that time, the British, whose tendency was to err on the conservative side, estimated that there were about 8,000 North Vietnamese troops in Laos. The American figure was 10,000.

In fact, the Vietnamese Communists hadn't left at all: they had merely withdrawn a token number of their men to conform with the reluctant admission that there might have been a few of them in Laos, almost, as it were, by inadvertence. For the rest, they simply continued to use Laos as and when they pleased, mainly for the purpose of supplying the Communist Viet Cong guerrillas in South Vietnam along what came to be known as the 'Ho Chi Minh trail'. A year after the Geneva settlement, there were forty to fifty Viet Cong technical experts integrated in each Pathet Lao battalion and no fewer than eleven North Vietnamese *regular* battalions ranging from northern to southern Laos along the Ho Chi Minh trail. Neutralist officers (under General Kong Lae) had recognized the faces of former Vietnamese military instructors, dressed as civilians and living with the Pathet Lao, and had monitored radio orders in Vietnamese. In the circumstances, it is hardly surprising that 'quiet Americans' started returning to Laos in various civilian capacities, or that American planes started air-dropping supplies to anti-Communist troops, notably the Meo tribesmen, who grew the opium the North Vietnamese coveted, and who were usefully anti-Vietnamese.

This is where Mr Khrushchev's famous 'troika' principle had led. It may be remembered that Mr Khrushchev had proposed that control of the United Nations should be vested in a triple secretariat in which Communists and Westerners should serve under a neutralist Secretary-General. The original control commissions set up after the 1954 Geneva conference had, in fact, embodied this principle in that they consisted of Poles and Canadians under Indian chairmanship. During the 1961–2 conference on Laos, the control commission (which the Laotian government had sent packing in 1958) was back in business. More significantly, the so-called government of national union was a triumphant example of the troika – a marriage of incompatibles that was guaranteed to frustrate administration and give the Communists further time to resume their military pressure.

This is exactly what happened. Once again, there was a reversal of alliances. General Kong Lae, who had been forced into an alliance with the Pathet Lao at the time of General Phoumi's *putsch* on Vientiane (see Part Three, Chapter 2), now improved his political education on contact with the Communists. One of his chief assistants, Colonel Deuane Sipaseuth, denouncing Kong Lae as a tool of the imperialists, broke away with a few hundred men calling themselves 'true neutralists' (to distinguish themselves from Kong Lae's, who were merely 'neutralists'). Kong Lae, caught between the suddenly hostile Pathet Lao and Deuane's force, made his peace with General Phoumi. This, too, was the chaos that is Laos.

Inevitably, the coalition broke down; in the spring of 1963, the two Pathet Lao ministers – our old acquaintances Souphannouvong and Phoumi Vongvichit – left Vientiane for the Communist areas, and didn't come back, although their seats were symbolically kept open for them, to preserve the fiction that the coalition remained in being.

Although Prince Souvanna Phouma managed, almost miraculously, to stay in power (if the expression is permissible), his government lurched from crisis to crisis. On 18 April 1964, an anti-Phoumi right-wing *junta*, headed by General Kouprasith Abhay, briefly seized power; but handed it back to the Prince a week later in the face of a concerted display of indignation from the Americans, British and Russians. At the end of February 1965, Phoumi's supporters tried to take revenge on Kouprasith, and heavy fighting broke out in Vientiane. Kouprasith's forces set fire to Phoumi's Vientiane house and Phoumi escaped to Siam. This was, as far as could be judged, the political end of Phoumi (who, in December 1966, was sentenced *in absentia* to 20 years' gaol). But it was not the end of Kouprasith's troubles, or of Prince Souvanna's. In October 1966, Brigadier-General Thao Ma, operational commander of the Laotian Air Force, who had a personal grievance against General Kouprasith, bombed the latter's headquarters. His coup – for this is what it was meant to be – failed, and General Ma also took refuge in Siam. As for Prince Souvanna, his attempts to merge the neutralist and rightist forces into one army provoked the anger of General Kong Lae, who resigned his command and went abroad in a huff. On 23 March 1967, he was replaced by Colonel Somphet.

Meanwhile, the war had developed just as though there had never been a Geneva settlement in 1962. In October 1965, the

Pathet Lao Fighting Forces were renamed 'People's Liberation Army', which brought them in line with Chinese and North Vietnamese styling. As the war in South Vietnam escalated, so did the number of North Vietnamese troops or other personnel in Laos. In the summer of 1966, US Intelligence reports suggested that North Vietnamese personnel in Laos, manning the 'Ho Chi Minh trail' or fighting alongside the Pathet Lao forces, might total as many as 70,000. On their side, the Americans intensified bombing operations against the Communist forces from January 1965 on.

In December 1967, joint North Vietnamese and Pathet Lao forces launched an offensive in southern Laos; shortly after, a complimentary offensive began in the north, where the Communists seized Nam Bac on 20 January 1968. This brought them to within 35 miles of Luang Prabang, the Royal capital. For the first time, North Vietnamese planes were in action over Laos. (These attacks were variously described as 'seasonal rice raids' and a 'war of the supply routes'.) Both phrases were applicable, but neither did justice to the wider perspective of Hanoi's designs on Laos, or the still wider one of 'revolutionary war' in action. Indeed, in January, just after the capture of Nam Bac, a delegation of the Havana-based Tricontinental Solidarity Organization – sometimes called the 'guerrillas' international' – was welcomed in communist-held Laos. Its members thus enjoyed a ringside seat at one of the triumphs of revolutionary war.

VIETNAM

If one swallows the fiction that what happened in Laos was a spontaneous uprising of the Laotian people, then one has to define the Laotian hostilities as a 'civil war'. Other countries are not supposed to intervene in a civil war. The North Vietnamese have gone on denying that they intervened and those who believe them must suppose them to be virtuous. The Chinese didn't intervene (except possibly on one occasion); and the Russians, when they did, were merely responding to the appeal of a government (Prince Souvanna Phouma's) which many countries recognized. So they, too, were virtuous. In this context, the Americans alone were trespassers, though all they had done was to send a few hundred advisers to help a government (Prince Boun Oum's) which they, and a number of other countries recognized as legal.

All this, however, was for the believers and the gullible. In fact, the North Vietnamese were in Laos before the Americans intervened; and they stayed on after the Americans had checked out.

If the North Vietnamese could get away with it in Laos – as they did – how much easier was it for them to get away with it in South Vietnam, which, after all, was only the other half of their own country. Psychologically, so many things were in Hanoi's favour. They had defeated the French and been deprived of the fruit of victory by the bargain struck by the great powers at Geneva in 1954. They had confidently looked forward to winning the general elections which (according to the unsigned final declaration of the Geneva conference) were supposed to be held throughout Vietnam in July 1956; but had been disappointed again because the Ngo Dinh Diem government in South Vietnam (which was not a party to the Geneva agreements) had refused to discuss election arrangements with them. On this issue, too, there was widespread sympathy for the North Vietnamese, who, in this instance, looked like the true democrats, since it was not they who were refusing elections. True, the South Vietnamese pointed out that elections were unlikely to be free in the North anyway; but few Westerners listened to them. Vietnam was a tiresome problem. It was supposed to have been 'settled' at Geneva. Now the South Vietnamese, with American backing, were upsetting everything with their stubborn refusal to face facts.

Years later, when the Americans had committed 15,000 men to South Vietnam, the North Vietnamese could still arouse sympathy. Wasn't this another civil war, beyond question this time, since Vietnamese were fighting Vietnamese? And weren't the Americans violating the Geneva agreements (to which they were not parties but which they had promised not to hinder) by their unprincipled intervention? As for the North Vietnamese, was it not a fact that they had not actually *invaded* South Vietnam in the sense of crossing the Geneva truce line?

Such questions seemed to answer themselves, and to exonerate Ho Chi Minh's Democratic Republic of Vietnam from all blame. But the evidence does not support this facile conclusion.

Let us take fundamentals first. It is true, of course, that Vietnamese are fighting Vietnamese south of the Geneva truce line. But this is no ordinary civil war. There are two duly constituted States in Vietnam. Questions of legitimacy apart, there is a northern republic and there is a southern republic, each with its supporters beyond Vietnam's boundaries. If, as I hope to show, the insurrection in South Vietnam is directed and controlled from North Vietnam, then the North is guilty of aggression, even though the bulk of General Giap's regular forces have remained on their side of the line.

Another fundamental point – a historical one – needs to be made at the outset. The Vietnamese are certainly one people, speaking the same language and with the same culture. But the circumstances of the Vietnamese drive to the south, the distance between Saigon and Hanoi, and the difficulty of pre-air age communications have all fostered separatist sentiment in the south. For about 200 years, until the close of the eighteenth century, Vietnam was divided into mutually hostile halves roughly coinciding with the present division. This, too, colours the view that the current troubles are just another civil war.

The second Indo-China war began much earlier than most people think: right at the beginning of 1958. Indeed, when it started, few people took much notice. There were raids on rubber estates and murders of village officials. Rebel bands were terrorizing the Cochinchinese countryside, especially in the Cambodian border region also due south of Saigon. It was difficult to find out what went on, both because the South Vietnamese authorities were chary of giving information and because the situation was confused. The Viet Minh were involved, but at that stage they were in a minority. Most of the insurgents belonged to one or other of those curious politico-religious sects that are peculiar to Cochinchina: Caodai, Hoa Hao, and Binh Xuyen. The Caodaists were adherents of a synthetic religion that combined elements of Buddhism, Confucianism, and Catholicism and had an unusual line in saints, including Victor Hugo. The Hoa Hao were a kind of non-conformist Buddhist sect founded in the 1930s by a man known as the Mad Bonze. There was nothing religious about the Binh Xuyen, although they were usually lumped with the other two. Starting as river pirates they had moved into Saigon and gained control first of gambling and prostitution; then, with Bao Dai's consent, of the police, which secured them immunity from the consequences of their own misdeeds. All three sects had private armies; and all three had played a part in the first Indo-China war. In the spring of 1955, Diem had smashed them, starting with the Binh Xuyen. Morality, at that time, was on his side. But it would have been good politics to keep on the right side of the Caodaists and Hoa Hao. Towards the end of 1957 the remnants of the sectarian armies dug up their hidden arms and took to battle.

So did the Viet Minh. The regulars had been evacuated to the North after Geneva – at least most of them had – but the irregulars stayed behind. Indeed most of them were Cochinchinese who simply went back to their villages. But they too had hidden arms. And they too dug them out.

At first the Viet Minh bands simply identified themselves with the Caodai and Hoa Hao. Soon enough, however, they were in control. It was history repeating itself. The methods used were much the same as those I have described in Part Two, Chapter 4. Murder and terrorism got rid of prying officials; coercion turned men and women into outlaws, and once they were in with the Communists there was no easy way out. Moreover, once in, the villagers were financially better off; for in return for food, shelter, and information, the Viet Cong, as they came to be known, offered the villagers 'exemption' from taxes to the Diem authorities and rents to landlords. The Viet Cong's own taxes were less onerous. Continually on the move, especially in the early days, the Viet Cong left behind threats of execution if orders were not carried out. Such threats were promptly followed up when the need arose.

By mid-1959 murders of officials averaged one a day and by March 1961 – on the eve of SEATO's Bankok meeting on Laos – twenty times that figure. The victims included ordinary peasants as well as government officials, village notables, and police. Though the bulk of the guerrillas were southerners, they were being directed by agents sent from the North either by junk along the coast or across Laos; there were also many guerrillas operating in South Vietnam but encamped in Cambodia where they took refuge when the southern army gave chase. By this time (early 1961) the Viet Cong numbered nearly 10,000 men; and by the end of the year, probably 20,000. In 1962, the number reached some 30,000 and this figure remained constant despite heavy losses, for as fast as the guerrillas died or were captured others took their places.

Throughout the second Indo-China war, Hanoi radio and the North Vietnamese party press has claimed that it was a spontaneous popular uprising against the oppressive Diem régime and against United States' attempts to turn South Vietnam into an aggressive military base in violation of the 1954 Geneva agreements. At times, however, the Lao Dong (Communist) Party has given the game away. Indeed the evidence of North Vietnamese direction and control of operations in South Vietnam is overwhelming. Much of it, of course, comes from the statements of captured Viet Cong personnel and seized documents. But there is a good deal of corroborative evidence in the speeches of North Vietnamese leaders and published records of party decisions.

As early as 10 July 1959, Ho Chi Minh himself, writing in the Belgian Communist journal *Red Flag*, had this to say:

We are building socialism in Vietnam, but we are building it only in one part of the country, while in the other part we still have to *direct and bring to a close the middle-class democratic and anti-imperialist revolution.*

The words I have italicized are interesting on more than one count. They clearly show that the Lao Dong Party intended to keep control of the insurrection in the south. They also show that the Communist direction of the movement was to be kept inconspicuous. Ostensibly, the revolution was to be a bourgeois one; in reality, it was to be controlled by the Communists who, when the time came, would come into the open and take over. This, in fact, was the classic Maoist pattern of revolution which the Vietnamese Communists themselves had followed when fighting the French. General Giap, in his collection of essays, *People's War, People's Army*, published in Hanoi in September 1961, described how the united front technique had brought the Communists to power in North Vietnam. He wrote:

The Vietnamese people's war of liberation was victorious because we had a wide and firm National United Front ...

organized and led by the party of the working class: the Indo-China Communist Party, now the Vietnam Workers' (Lao Dong) Party.

By the time these words appeared, the Lao Dong had long set up a 'front' in South Vietnam, with the object of lending credibility to its claim that this was a broadly based popular uprising. The decision to set it up was taken at the crucial National Congress of the Lao Dong Party in Hanoi in September 1960. On 10 September, the congress passed a long resolution, from which I quote the following passage:

In the present stage, the Vietnamese revolution has two strategic tasks - first, to carry out the socialist revolution in North Vietnam; second, to liberate South Vietnam from the ruling yoke of the U.S. imperialists and their henchmen in order to achieve national unity and complete independence and freedom throughout the country. . . .
To ensure the complete success of the revolutionary struggle in South Vietnam our people there must strive to establish a united bloc of workers, peasants, and soldiers and to bring into being a broad national united front directed against the U.S.–Diem clique and based on the worker-peasant alliance.

Three months later, in December, Hanoi announced the creation of the National Front for the Liberation of South Vietnam (NFLSV). It was a clear case of orders received and carried out.

What was the NFLSV and whom did it represent? At first it was difficult even to invent an answer. But in time the story came out in dribs and drabs from Hanoi and Peking radios. In the first instance, the Front represented the Communists; rather more openly, indeed, than had the Lien Viet and Viet Minh, those earlier Vietnamese Communist fronts. In January 1962 an openly Communist party, the People's Revolutionary Party, was set up in South Vietnam. The PRP's manifesto admitted its descent from the Indo-Chinese Communist Party and the Lao Dong. That it was intended to provide the leadership of the NFLSV was not in doubt, for on 4 April, the Lao Dong's newspaper, *Nhan Dan*, published a statement attributed to the PRP saying:

The Vietnamese Revolutionary People's Party volunteers to act as the assault soldier in the front line of this struggle.

A front that openly represented only the Communists would not, however, fulfil its purpose. So at intervals Hanoi reported the formation of no fewer than fourteen parties and organizations in South Vietnam, bodies with names like the Radical Socialist Party, the Vietnam People's Revolutionary Party, the Peasants' Union for Liberation, the Association of Patriotic and Democratic Journalists, the Vietnamese Nationals of Chinese Origin, etc. It is just possible that one or two of these bodies may have existed independently of the Lao Dong, but most of them were obviously puppets manipulated from Hanoi. They were supposed to constitute the Front, but most of them did not come into being (by courtesy of Hanoi radio) until *after* the Front had been formed. Several of them shared the same officials. A good example is that of Nguyen Van Hieu. Hanoi broadcast a biography of him on 16 April 1962. He was described as Secretary-General of the NFLSV *and* of the Radical Socialist Party *and* of the South Vietnam Committee for the Defence of World Peace. In July 1962, however, he turned up in Moscow as Vice-Chairman of the South Vietnamese Committee for the Defence of World Peace; and in August he went to Budapest as Vice-President of the Association of Patriotic and Democratic Journalists. A busy man.

The fourteen 'organizations' were said to have met somewhere in South Vietnam from 16 February to 3 March 1962 in what Hanoi and Peking radios later described as the First Congress of the NFLSV. But it was not till 13 April that Hanoi broadcast the Front's policy statement. This clearly followed the line laid down by the Lao Dong congress in September 1960. It envisaged the formation of a 'broad national democratic administration in South Vietnam' which, once in power, would release political prisoners, guarantee freedom for all parties, accept aid from all countries, proclaim a policy of neutrality according to the Bandung principles, and 'advance peaceful reunification'. These points included liberties that were more, far more, than the people of North Vietnam can expect from their own government; but the sting was in the tail: once the

South was reunited 'peacefully' with North Vietnam, Communism and the denial of civil rights would extend over the whole of Vietnam. This, however, was not stated in the Front's programme.

In May, just a few weeks after the Front's programme had been published, the International Control Commission (ICC) in Vietnam came out with clear evidence that North Vietnam was violating the Geneva agreements by sending arms and men into South Vietnam. It was the first time this body, set up to administer the Geneva truce, had been so outspoken. The Polish delegates automatically vetoed any mention of Communist misdeeds and until then the Indian chairman had usually overruled the Canadian members who would have liked such evidence brought to light. This time, perhaps because of the deterioration of relations between India and China, the Indian members of the ICC decided that the evidence should be published. And though the Polish members dissented and brought out a minority report of their own, the case against North Vietnam was damaging. Here are the passages in which the report summarized the ICC's findings:

In specific instances there is evidence to show that armed and unarmed personnel, arms, munitions, and other supplies have been sent from the Zone in the North [North Vietnam] to the Zone in the South [South Vietnam] with the object of supporting, organizing, and carrying out hostile activities, including armed attacks, directed against the armed forces and administration of the Zone in the South. . . .

The Committee has come to the further conclusion that there is evidence to show that the PAVN (the North Vietnam People's Army) has allowed the Zone in the North to be used for inciting, encouraging, and supporting hostile activities in the Zone in the South, aimed at the overthrow of the administration in the South.

The ICC's report went to the British and Soviet Foreign Ministers as 'co-chairmen' of the Geneva conference. Immediately Hanoi's radio, press, and leaders let out a concerted howl of denunciation, accusing India of every kind of imperialist outrage. But the truth was out and no amount of abuse could hide it. North Vietnam's elaborate smokescreen had been dispersed.

Long before the ICC had made its report, however, the southern intelligence service and its American advisers had built up a full picture of North Vietnamese intervention in the South. The evidence was published by the American State Department in December 1961 in the form of a blue book in two parts, entitled *A Threat to the Peace: North Vietnam's Effort to Conquer South Vietnam*. The first part of this report outlined the conclusions to be drawn from the evidence, and the second consisted of appendices containing photo-copies of statements made by captured Viet Cong personnel and other supporting documents. At the time, owing to the American military involvement in South Vietnam, this evidence was largely overlooked or discontinued. But the ICC's report provided triumphant confirmation of its accuracy.

One of the American report's most interesting disclosures was the existence of a special 'Committee for Supervision of the South', an offshoot of the Lao Dong central committee, which directs the activities of the Viet Cong under cover of the National Front. At the service of these bodies is the vast and highly organized intelligence network of Hanoi's Central Research Agency or CRA (Cuc Nghien-Cuu Trung-Uong). According to the State Department's report of 1961, the CRA's operation in South Vietnam is 'one of the most extensive of its kind on the world'.

A piece of evidence that emerged too late for inclusion in the State Department or ICC reports was a document that fell into the South Vietnamese Army's hands in the autumn of 1962. This was a Communist directive to party provincial committees in South Vietnam. Not unnaturally this document, which was not intended for publication, was franker than others that were. Indeed it set out to answer the misgivings of unsophisticated local Communists who were bewildered by orders to associate with non-Communists within the NFLSV. Two particularly damaging passages were these:

Party Central (the Lao Dong's central committee) had to introduce the tactic of the Front and to create the NFLSV with the object of attracting into its ranks capitalist and intellectual classes, including the capitalist youth, students, and intellectuals of the cities and the middle and rich farmers of the countryside.

The policy of the (Communist) Party is nothing more than a tactic appropriate to the present stage. When the revolution to liberate South Vietnam has achieved victory, that policy will be altered. At that moment our Party will proclaim itself by its actions, for it will play the leading part in a proletarian revolution in South Vietnam.

By its own mouth, the Lao Dong stood condemned.

More recently still, towards the end of 1965, it became known that the Viet Cong's political controlling body, the NFLSV, was set up by Le Duan, who is now the first secretary of the Lao Dong party. Although the formal decision to set up the Front was not taken until September 1960, the decision to 'liberate' the South by force was reached earlier, in May 1959. By this time, however, the northern ruling party had sent Le Duan secretly to the South to unify and reorganize the Viet Minh insurgents under Communist control. The fact that it was Le Duan who went is itself of great importance. Le Duan had commanded the Viet Minh guerrillas in the South in the latter stages of the first Indo-China war. He had fiercely opposed the Geneva settlement as a 'betrayal' of the Vietnamese people. When President Diem refused to discuss election arrangements with North Vietnam, Le Duan argued that he had been right all along; and later he got his way about starting up a new 'liberation' war and was sent south of the Geneva truce line late in 1957 to organize it, returning to Hanoi in 1958.

One of the most important consequences of this turn of events is that as the second war has waxed, so has the power of Le Duan, so that today this partisan of war to the bitter end has become the most powerful man in North Vietnam. True, as these lines were written, Ho Chi Minh was still President and Chairman of the Party; but Ho is old and, some say, showing signs of senility. The man who determines policy is probably Le Duan; and unless and until he is dislodged, the war will go on.

Despite all this, a number of western writers and speakers have continued to argue that the Viet Cong is essentially an autonomous Southern body, even if its dominant element is Communist; that it would survive even if support from the North were withdrawn; and that the proper way of bringing the second Indo-China war to an end is to negotiate with the Viet Cong, not with Hanoi. Many of those who use these arguments do so either in ignorance or in bad faith, but the late Professor Bernard Fall, who used them in the American quarterly *Foreign Affairs* for October 1966, cannot be charged with either. Some months after Professor Fall's article appeared, and just after his own death in an anti-Viet Cong action in March 1967, fresh documents came to light that might, conceivably, have caused him to modify his thesis, had he lived to study them.

The documents were captured in the spring of 1967 when a large Viet Cong headquarters was taken by American forces. Three of them were of outstanding importance. One was a long letter from Le Duan – mentioned above – to the current overall commander of the Viet Cong in South Vietnam, Nguyen Chi Thanh, himself a member of the North Vietnam party's polit-buro. The other two documents were Viet Cong notebooks recording a lecture given by General Nguyen Van Vinh, Deputy Chief of Staff of the North Vietnam Army. Both Le Duan's letter and General Vinh's lecture appear to date from the late spring or early summer of 1966; but other documents captured at the same time make it quite clear that the situation they revealed has not changed.

Le Duan's letter and General Vinh's lecture both arose out of the 12th plenum of the Lao Dong party in March 1966. In the name of resolutions passed on that occasion, both men issued directives to the Viet Cong on the conduct of the war, naming objectives and defining the conditions under which peace negotiations were to be initiated. It was made clear that there should be no negotiations until military superiority had been achieved, even if this took years. 'It is possible,' said General Vinh, 'that the North conducts negotiations while the South continues fighting, and that the South also participates in negotiations while continuing to fight.'

MOTIVES IN HANOI

There are specific reasons for Ho Chi Minh's military pressures in Laos and South Vietnam, as well as the more general ones of

Vietnam's historical drive southward and Ho's own ambitions. One reason is food; another, the desire to avoid satellization by China; and yet another, the foreign exchange profits from the opium grown in northern Laos. North Vietnam has always been a food deficit area, while the South, in normal times, has a rice surplus for export. In 1961, North Vietnam launched a five-year plan with a food crops target of $9\frac{1}{2}$ million tons, including seven million tons of rice. But bad weather and Communist methods kept the rice figure persistently low and in 1962 the party cut the 1965 total food target to only just over seven million tons.

If North Vietnam controlled South Vietnam, this perennial food problem would not arise, that is, unless the usual Communist mismanagement of land questions produced the old familiar shortages. More important still, if North Vietnam controlled the South and, if possible, Laos and Cambodia as well, it would come up in the world. It would no longer be a minor Communist power, but a middle power, standing on its own feet without Soviet or Chinese support and able, within limits, to have its own foreign policy – perhaps with French help, as General de Gaulle has hinted.

For years, Ho Chi Minh managed to keep his party out of the Sino-Soviet dispute. But when the partial Test Ban Treaty was signed in Moscow in the summer of 1963, it had to choose and opted for China – the giant on the doorstep. This must have been deeply distasteful to Ho, both as a Vietnamese nationalist and as a politician who knows the value of playing off one side against the other. Indeed there are signs that the issue led to a crisis within the Lao Dong Party, with General Giap and the Premier, Pham Van Dong, on the pro-Soviet side, and Truong Chinh (whom we have met earlier) on the pro-Chinese side, with Ho reluctantly siding with Truong Chinh.

From February 1965, however, Ho Chi Minh was able to resume his favourite posture of equilibrium between the two Communist giants. It was at this stage that the war began to escalate in earnest, and it was evident that Russia easily outstripped China as a supplier of modern war weapons, including SAM missiles and MiG 21s.

Despite North Vietnam's heavy dependence on Chinese good-will and Soviet supplies, it is clear that the initiative has all along been with North Vietnam. It is quite wrong to assume, as many people have, that China calls the tune in Indo-China. Paradoxically, although the Chinese would like to get the Americans out of Laos and Vietnam and doubtless approve of North Vietnamese efforts to this end, they would probably not be too happy if Ho Chi Minh fulfilled all his original ambitions, bringing most of Indo-China under Vietnamese leadership and making Vietnam economically independent of China.

CAMBODIA

The North Vietnamese Communists have been far less active in Cambodia than in Laos or South Vietnam. This is hardly for lack of desire, but for more practical reasons. One is that they have been too deeply engaged in the other two Indo-China States which geography has made more accessible from North Vietnam. Another is that, as we have seen, Cambodia emerged from the 1954 Geneva settlement with its territory intact. Yet another reason lies in the dynamism and appeal of Prince Sihanouk, the Cambodian Head of State.

Prince Sihanouk has, however, more than once blamed the Viet Minh for subversive challenges to his authority from the local Cambodian Communist Party, known as the Pracheachon. In April 1960 he wrote an article in the Phom Penh paper, *The Nationalist*, describing a Communist plot to infiltrate the Prince's Sangkum party awaiting a suitable time to destroy his régime. The evidence, he wrote, was contained in documents found on a captured Viet Minh agent. These clearly showed collusion between the Viet Minh and Pracheachon. In May 1962 fourteen members of the Pracheachon were sentenced to death in Pnom Penh for further subversive activities.

Prince Sihanouk has always been careful to distinguish the Vietnamese Communists from the Chinese or Soviet Communists. He has had occasional tussles with the Russians, but by and large he has drawn continually closer to China during the past four years. This has been due partly to an almost fatalistic view, which he has frequently expressed in public, that China is bound eventually to dominate at least continental South-East Asia, but even more to a growing exasperation with United States and, to a lesser extent, British policy. In January 1959 Prince Sihanouk announced details of plots against him by the discredited Son Ngoc Thanh and others. The plotters were said to have been operating from Siam – an ally of America's – and South Vietnam, which was under American protection. The plots fanned old troubles between Cambodia and its neighbours arising out of such contentions as Siam's border claims, the treatment of the Cambodian minority in South Vietnam, a disputed temple on the Siamese–Cambodian border (which the World Court eventually awarded to Cambodia), South Vietnam's claim to a group of islands in the Gulf of Siam, an anti-Sihanouk radio station, said to be operating from South Vietnam, and repeated clashes between Cambodian troops and the better-armed South Vietnamese pursuing Viet Cong guerillas across the Cambodian border. As time went on, the Prince increasingly blamed all these causes of friction on the Americans – for failing to keep the Siamese and South Vietnamese in order. And the British were blamed for indifference if not positive sympathy with Cambodia's enemies.

In August 1962 Prince Sihanouk proposed that the fourteen nations that had just settled the fate of Laos – at least on paper – should meet again to guarantee Cambodia's neutrality and integrity. Since the Communist powers stood to gain by another chance of slanging the Americans over the behaviour of their small South-East Asian friends, they accepted the Prince's proposal. General de Gaulle, well set in his anti-American mood, also endorsed it. But the British had no taste for another lengthy wrangle with the Communists. And the Americans had no wish to expose themselves and their friends to attacks from the Cambodians and Communists. The British and Americans therefore proposed that the Prince should first try to settle his differences with Siam and South Vietnam through bilateral talks.

This Anglo-Saxon reluctance infuriated the Prince, whose anger finally boiled over late in 1963. On 5 November he said

147

he would renounce American aid and call in Chinese constitutional advisers if the anti-Sihanouk radio stations did not go
off the air by the end of the year. On 13 and 14 December
respectively, he recalled his ambassadors from Washington and
London. He then turned to France for aid to compensate for the
loss of the aid he had been getting from America.

None of this could immunize Cambodia against Vietnamese
Communists. Early in 1967, Communist guerillas were active
again and in April Prince Sihanouk publicly linked the so-called
Khmer rouges, who had been terrorizing Cambodian villages,
with the Viet Minh. This signalled a cooling of Cambodia's
relations with China. In September, Sihanouk dismissed two
left-wing ministers, who were linked with the *Khmers Rouges*,
for having become 'servants of China'.

More trouble followed. On 27 January 1968, Prince
Sihanouk blamed Vietnamese, Thai and Chinese Communists
for a new revolt in Battambang province, adjoining Thailand.
On 1 February he declared that a movement was afoot among
the mountain tribes of the Khmer Loeu area of north-eastern
Cambodia to set up a breakaway state under Vietnamese Communist control. These announcements were the more remark-
able because of the Prince's consistent policy of good relations
with the Vietnamese Communist movement, both in North and
South Vietnam. Indeed, his denunciations of Vietnamese
Communist actions against Cambodia did not prevent him from
sending greetings telegrams to Pham Van Dong, the North
Vietnamese Prime Minister, and to the National Liberation
Front in South Vietnam, on the occasion of the Tet or Vietnamese New Year festival. It has become harder than ever for
Sihanouk to stay neutral.

On 11 August 1966, the Indonesian and Malaysian Foreign Ministers met in Djakarta and signed an agreement ending the three-year 'confrontation' between their two countries. For President Sukarno, who was not present at the signing ceremony, this was the end of the neo-imperialist road. For South-East Asia, it was the end of the most unnecessary of its crises. To the happy end, Sukarno had done his worst to frustrate and delay a solution. The 'confronting' Foreign Ministers, Mr Adam Malik of Indonesia and Tun Abdul Razak of Malaysia, had signed a provisional agreement in Bangkok on 1 June. But Sukarno had gone on denouncing Malaysia as a 'Necolim' project – using his slogan word for *Neo*-colonialism, *Col*onialism and Imperialism.

The days of Sukarno's power had gone, however, and with them his chance of reviving Java's imperial past. For years, his office wall had been adorned by a map of the Madjapahit empire which, according to the most imaginative traditional accounts, included parts of the Philippines, the whole of New Guinea and Borneo, the Malay peninsula and the intervening islands. Was Madjapahit so vast ? Certainly this was the picture of it that was drawn by the Buddhist monk Prapantja in his poem *Nagarakertagama* in 1365. But Prapantja's poem is probably no more reliable a guide to history than Homer's *Iliad*. A number of modern scholars have tended to reduce the Madjapahit empire to central and eastern Java, Bali, and the island of Madura. Whatever the boundaries, however, Madjapahit had been, in Sukarno's eyes, a symbol of past glories and a beacon for future ones.

Let us return for a moment to the 1945 conference of the Japanese-sponsored Investigating Committee for the Preparation of Indonesia's Independence (Part Four, Chapter 1). It was there that Sukarno referred to Madjapahit and expressed territorial aspirations which the more moderate Dr Hatta disclaimed. Sukarno was not, however, the only speaker who spoke in this vein before the Investigating Committee, nor even the most extreme. Opening the Committee's first plenary session on 31 May 1945, Professor Mohammed Yamin had gone even further in staking claims on neighbouring lands. For instance he claimed Portuguese Timor as well as North Borneo on the ground that 'ever since the beginning of history, they have been inhabited by the people of Indonesia, forming part of our motherland'. He also claimed that the Papuans were of the same race as the Indonesians – a fantasy which Dr Hatta dismissed.

Later, Professor Yamin (who died in 1962) wrote a biography of Gadja Mada – the Javanese statesman who brought Madjapahit under centralized control – in which he sang the praises of the empire's social, cultural, and administrative achievements. When the Indonesian Nationalists opened a new university at Jogjakarta in 1947, they named it after Gadja Mada. Professor Yamin was, in fact, documenting a theory popular among Indonesian nationalists that Indonesia had enjoyed a golden age six or seven hundred years earlier, which was followed by the long darkness of Dutch rule. Sukarno himself subscribed to the golden age theory, and pledged himself to restore it.

There were several Sukarnos: a pleasure-lover who insisted on a quota of girls at home and abroad; a spell-binding demagogue whose capacity to achieve union with vast crowds was the real secret of his power; and a subtle politician, adept at balancing one set of opponents against another to his own benefit. Adept also at the 'one thing at a time' technique which, in their day, served Hitler and Stalin so well.

This last point is one reason why Sukarno buried his dream of empire for many years. Another reason was that in the years of nationalist struggle against the Dutch (1945–9) and after that until he parted company with Dr Hatta (1956), his power was by no means absolute. By and large the politicians who ran Indonesian affairs for the first few years after the transfer of sovereignty from the Dutch (December 1949) were more interested in setting up a viable State than in pressing nationalist claims. In January 1950, Mohammed Yamin publicly declared that Indonesia would not be 'complete' until it included the whole of New Guinea, British Borneo, and Portuguese Timor, and he was promptly repudiated by the Indonesian government. At that time, however, Vice-President Hatta was in office as Prime Minister and his effective power was greater than Sukarno's. Hatta, it will be remembered, had dissented from Yamin's and Sukarno's views at the Investigating Committee's meetings in 1945; and Sukarno had agreed with Yamin. Though Sukarno did not publicly claim British Borneo after independence, later events showed that he had not changed his mind.

On one issue, however, all the Indonesian politicians were agreed: Dutch New Guinea should be transferred to Indonesia. Even Hatta, who had dissented from Yamin's view that the Papuans were racially akin to the Indonesians, agreed with his colleagues on this point. It is time we looked at the Indonesian claim to West New Guinea.

Irian Barat or West Irian, as the Indonesians call it, is a vast and inhospitable place inhabited by some 700,000 Stone-Age Melanesians who have nothing in common with the Indonesians and speak about 200 mutually incomprehensible dialects. Despite Professor Yamin's ramblings, the Indonesian claim was based not on alleged racial affinity but on historical and legal grounds. The main basis for the claim was that Indonesia was the successor State to the Netherlands East Indies and that the latter's entire territory should therefore be handed over to Indonesia. The Indonesians argued that since West Irian had been administered as part of the Moluccas – which, in turn, were part of the East Indies – it could not be withheld by the Dutch when they transferred sovereignty. To this, the Dutch reply was that West New Guinea was a backward area, toward whose primitive, non-Indonesian people they felt a special sense of obligation. The Charter of Transfer of Sovereignty – to which the Indonesians were a party – did, in fact, treat West New Guinea as a special case. Article 1 transferred 'complete sovereignty over Indonesia' to the then Republic of the United States of Indonesia; but Article 2 stipulated that the *status quo* was to be maintained in West New Guinea pending negotiations to determine its political status, which were to take place within one year.

The legal position was thus ambiguous. The moral issue could be looked at in different ways, according to the colour of one's skin. Clearly West Irian under the Dutch was a colony. But wouldn't it be just as much a colony under Indonesian rule? The people of West Irian were Papuans, ethnically identical with the people of eastern New Guinea, who were under Australian rule. Surely the fairest thing would have been to bring all the people of New Guinea – east and west – simultaneously to the stage of self-government and independence. And indeed the Dutch and Australian government announced a joint policy to this end in November 1957.

But the Indonesians argued that although it was 'colonialism' for Papuans to be ruled by white Dutchmen, it would not be colonialism for Papuans to be ruled by brown Indonesians. This was one way of putting it. Another way is that neo-imperialism is no more concerned with the inherent rights of subject peoples than any other kind of imperialism. The Indonesians, whipped into irredentist fury by Sukarno, were determined to get West Irian. And of course they did get it, in May 1963, by a combination of economic, military, and diplomatic pressures. To placate the Dutch and world opinion, the Indonesians did promise, however, that a referendum would be held not later than 1969, giving the Papuans a choice between independence and incorporation into Indonesia. *But Sukarno later repudiated this pledge.* Whether they wanted it or not, the Papuans were now subjects of his empire.

It was frustrating for Sukarno that Indonesia fell short of being a great power despite its 100 million people, or more, inhabiting richly-endowed islands spanning 3,000 miles, and its well-equipped army of 350,000 men. Indeed it would be much closer to being a great power if Sukarno had devoted as much energy to developing the country, balancing its budget, and seeing that it was honestly and efficiently administered as he did to the personal pursuit of pleasure and to dramatizing his dream of empire.

Sitting in his office in Merdeka Palace, and looking at the map of Indonesia's past, he probably felt that only two things stood in the way of his ultimate ambitions: the British base in Singapore and the American bases in the Philippines. One does not have to look any farther for his fury over Malaysia. Sukarno's fury, however, was carefully rationed. It exploded at pre-determined times, as the history of his 'confrontation' against Malaysia clearly shows.

Let us see first how Malaysia came into being. On economic and geographical grounds, it always seemed desirable that Malaya and Singapore should merge. Economically, Singapore is the trading entrepôt for Malaya; geographically, it is Malaya's prolongation. But for a long time, the Malayan Prime Minister, Tunku Abdul Rahman, wouldn't hear of a merger. In Malaya, the Malays outnumbered the Chinese, but in Singapore the Chinese had an overwhelming majority. In a straight merger between Malaya and Singapore, the Malays would have been out-numbered. This was one reason for the Tunku's reluctance; another was his fear of the Communist element in Singapore. When Malaya became independent in 1957, Singapore's up-and-coming People's Action Party (PAP), led by Mr Lee Kuan-yew, was deeply infiltrated by Communists. The Tunku had no desire to take over Singapore's security problem as well as his own. He was quite happy for the British to stay on and take care of security on the island. Apart from this, there was and is a certain incompatibility of temperament between the Tunku and Mr Lee. Although both were barristers, the Tunku had taken his finals late in life, while Mr Lee, with a 'first' at Cambridge, had had a brilliant academic career. The Tunku, no intellectual, imposed himself by personal charm, good humour, and common sense. Mr Lee, possessed of one of the best intellects in South-East Asia, calculates his moves long in advance. Again, Mr Lee is a Chinese and the Tunku a Malay; and the Tunku is twenty-one years older than Mr Lee, who is in his forties.

From the British point of view, the Tunku's distaste for a merger with Singapore was a nuisance. The Singapore base still looked essential for South-East Asian defence in its wide aspects. Given Singapore's Communist problem, it therefore seemed unwise to cast Singapore adrift into independence, quite apart from the economic and geographical considerations. For these reasons, the British were willing to offer Singapore only internal self-government, not independence. The new self-governing State of Singapore was born on 3 June 1959, foreign affairs and defence remaining under British control, while an Internal Security Council was set up with Malayan partici-pation. Four days earlier, Mr Lee's People's Action Party had won forty-three of the fifty-one seats in Singapore's Legislative Assembly.

Mr Lee had campaigned on a frankly anti-colonialist plat-form, which had scared the British business community but had brought him support from the extreme Left, including the Communists. After a year in power, the PAP started disinte-grating. In a remarkable series of broadcasts in 1961, Mr Lee castigated the underhand tactics of the Communists, who had tried to gain control of his party from within. By that time, the Communists and the wilder anti-colonialists of the PAP had deserted Mr Lee or been expelled, and his position in parliament was weakening. The Tunku, watching these events from Kuala Lumpur, came to feel that it would be more dangerous to Malaya's security to allow Singapore to drift into Communist hands on its own than to agree to a merger and have a stronger say in Singapore's affairs. But he thought the risks of the merger would be still further reduced if the British Borneo territories were also brought in, to form a wider federation. This was always a debatable point, since the Chinese of Borneo together with those of Singapore and Malaya, would still out-number the Malays. But there was a strong Malaysian element in the Borneo populations, consisting of Dusuns, Dayaks, and other related tribes, and the Tunku counted on these to reduce Chinese influence. This is how the Greater Malaysia plan (as it was known at first) came to be launched by the Tunku, in a speech in Singapore on 27 May 1961. As originally envisaged, the Federation was to consist of Malaya, Singapore, and the three territories of British Borneo: North Borneo, Brunei, and Sarawak. The Sultan of Brunei, however, later declined to join in, and Singapore has now seceded, so that the Federation has shrunk to Malaya, Sabah (North Borneo), and Sarawak.

Sukarno didn't decide he was furious about Malaysia until early in 1963. Indeed on 20 November 1961 – six months after Tunku Abdul Rahman's first announcement – the Indonesian Foreign Minister, Dr Subandrio, welcomed the proposed Federation in a speech before the U.N. General Assembly, in which he said:

We are not only disclaiming the territories outside the former Netherlands East Indies, though they are of the same island (i.e. Borneo, the rest of which belongs to Indonesia), but – more than that – when Malaya told us of its intention to merge with . . . Sarawak, Brunei, and North Borneo as one federation, we told them we had no objections and that we wished them success with this merger so that everyone might live in peace and freedom.

Bringing the various parts of Malaysia together was not easy and took a long time. There were many and complicated negotiations between the territories concerned and between them and Britain. There was a British Commission of Inquiry in Borneo which published its findings in June 1962; there was a referendum on Malaysia in Singapore in September that year. Yet throughout this period, the Indonesians had no fault to find with Malaysia. Then towards the end of December 1962, the Indonesian Communist Party (PKI) started the ball rolling by denouncing Malaysia as 'a new concentration of colonial forces on the very frontiers of our country'. Indonesian government spokesmen, finding the ball at their feet, picked it up. And on 23 February 1963 President Sukarno himself gave it a mighty kick, declaring that Malaysia was a neo-colonialist design for the protection of imperialist economic privileges. It had thus

taken Sukarno nearly two years, from the date of Tunku Abdul
Rahman's first announcement, to decide he was furious about
Malaysia. Why did it take him so long?

The course of events suggests that Sukarno's empire-building
had a time-table. Top priority was obviously to be given to West
New Guinea, the unfinished business left over from the Round
Table conference with the Dutch in 1949, on which all Indonesians seemed to agree. At the time when Dr Subandrio was
making his U.N. speech wishing success to Malaysia, Sukarno
was preparing to launch his 'final campaign for the recovery of
West Irian'. This was clearly not a good time to take on Britain
and Malaya. But in August 1962 the Dutch agreed to transfer
West New Guinea to Indonesia after an interim period of U.N.
administration. The way was then clear – or almost – to start
applying pressure on the British and Malaysians.

There was at that time only one more event to wait for: the
referendum on Malaysia which Singapore's Prime Minister, Mr
Lee Kuan-yew, was to hold in September. There was at least a
possibility that the results would be embarrassing to Mr Lee's
government, perhaps to the extent of hindering or delaying the
final negotiations on Malaysia. For opposition to Malaysia was
considerable within Singapore – not, it is true, because more
than a handful of Singaporeans supported Sukarno's imperial
ambitions; but because the well-organized Chinese Communist
element was against anything (such as a merger with Malaya)
that would improve the capacity of the authorities to keep them
in order. In the event, however, seventy-one per cent of those
who took part in the referendum declared themselves in favour
of Mr Lee's proposals for joining the proposed Federation of
Malaysia. The Communists and their supporters had appealed
to the voters to show their opposition to Malaysia by casting
blank papers. Just over twenty-five per cent of those who took
part did so. This showed how strong the opposition was; but
more significantly, it showed that the great majority of the
people of Singapore were against Communist arguments and
Indonesian pretensions.

Now President Sukarno felt he could really launch his campaign to frustrate the creation of Malaysia, and, for a start, to

gain control of the British territories of Borneo. The instrument for the execution of this policy was at hand, in the form of A. M. Azahari, a Brunei politician of mixed Arab-Malay descent. Azahari was a frustrated man; his Brunei People's Party had won all the elective seats in Brunei's elections in August 1962 but was unable to form a government because its members were outnumbered in the Legislative Assembly by the officially-nominated members. On 8 December, Azahari's followers, calling themselves the North Kalimantan Liberation Army, launched a revolt in Brunei.

Azahari's revolt was soon suppressed and it need not concern us too deeply here. More relevant was Azahari's background and his usefulness to Indonesia. When he launched his abortive rebellion he proclaimed himself Prime Minister of a 'Revolutionary State of North Kalimantan' and made it clear that he intended his army to 'liberate' not only Brunei, but Sarawak and North Borneo as well and unite them as one State. His choice of a name for his mythical State was arresting: Kalimantan is the Indonesian name for Borneo. Had his rebellion succeeded, what could be more natural than for his North Kalimantan State to federate with (that is, be swallowed by) Indonesian Kalimantan and the rest of Indonesia? In fact, Azahari's force had been trained by the Indonesian army in Indonesian Borneo.

In itself, Azahari's movement was not very important. But Indonesia soon recognized his government, which was allowed to operate in Djakarta *and*, for good measure, to keep a diplomatic mission there.

After the Brunei revolt, Sukarno does not seem to have been interested at any stage in a negotiated settlement of his differences with Tunku Abdul Rahman, except on his own terms. There were several attempts at negotiations, notably at Manila at the end of July 1963 when the two leaders met, with President Macapagal of the Philippines as host. The Tunku made a major concession at Manila by agreeing to postpone the proclaimation of Malaysia until after the U.N.'s Secretary-General had ascertained the wishes of the peoples of Sabah (North

Borneo) and Sarawak. Apparently mollified, President Sukarno joined President Macapagal and the Tunku in agreeing to set up a confederation of their three States, to be known as Maphilindo from the first syllables of Malaya, the Philippines, and Indonesia. U Thant, the U.N. Secretary-General, subsequently sent an international team of fact-finders to Borneo and its report, published on 14 September, was a sweeping vindication of the view that the peoples of Sabah and Sarawak understood what Malaysia was and supported it. This was not, however, what the Indonesians wanted to hear. On 15 September, the Indonesian cabinet denounced Malaysia as illegal and said it could not be recognized. On the 16th, Malaysia was proclaimed. And two days later, a carefully drilled mob in Djakarta burned the British embassy to the ground.

In any case, President Sukarno was playing a 'heads I win, tails you lose' game. If Maphilindo ever got off the ground (as it might, in time), his dream of empire would look like coming true. It is hard to conceive any other outcome of a confederal experiment in which Malaysia's eleven million people and the Philippines' thirty million joined with 100 million Indonesians. But 'confrontation' (that is, hostility towards Malaysia) went on anyway. It was more than just a war of nerves, though it was that, too. Hardly a week passed without a speech from Sukarno threatening to 'crush' Malaysia. But there was violence as well, in conditions ideally suited to hit-and-run attacks.

The frontiers between the Malaysian territories of Borneo and Indonesian Kalimantan run along nearly 1,000 miles of primary jungle. By the end of 1963, 12,000 men were being trained, on the Indonesian side, in terrorist tactics, guerrilla fighting, and sabotage. Many of them were members of Azahari's army, which, shortly after the failure of his revolt, was being referred to in Indonesian broadcasts as the *Tentara Nasional Kalimantan Utara* or TNKU (National Army of North Borneo). Azahari himself had lost control of the TNKU to the Indonesians. As with the Viet Cong and the Pathet Lao in Laos, the TNKU in Borneo was stiffened with, if not directed by, 'volunteers' from Indonesia's own National Army (*Tentara Nasional Indonesia* or TNI).

Azahari's original objective – Brunei – was no longer being attacked. The main targets were in Sarawak and Sabah. The main purpose of Indonesian raids across the border seemed to be to disrupt village life and overawe the inhabitants. Terrorists swooped on villages, looting the bazaar, kidnapping the head-man, and making propaganda speeches to audiences made aware of the invaders' weapons.

Sabah and Sarawak were not the only parts of Malaysia under threat from Indonesia. On 18 December 1963 Tunku Abdul Rahman of Malaya and Mr Lee Kuan-yew of Singapore gave details of Indonesian acts of war or subversion elsewhere, in statements to their respective parliaments. The Tunku men-tioned Indonesian plans to land battalions in Singapore, Johore, and Kelantan. The Indonesians, he said, had set up an organi-zation on the Rhio group of islands south of Singapore, under the former assistant Indonesian naval attaché in Singapore, Lieutenant Bambang Partono. A network of agents in Malaya and Singapore were said to be under his control.

Mr Lee's disclosures were more interesting still, for they threw light on an aspect of Sukarno's hypocrisy that had been overlooked. It was in May 1961, said Mr Lee, that Indonesia had made its first attempts to set up a subversive organization in Singapore. This was just before the Tunku made his first public reference to Malaysia and long before Indonesia officially decided to be hostile towards Malaya or Singapore. Indonesian agents set up a business house supposedly engaged in commerce but in reality to provide cover for intelligence and sabotage activities. Later two more such enterprises were established in Singapore. When Mr Lee spoke, Singapore had been puzzled, perhaps rather than terrorized, for some time by sporadic explosions in streets and public parks. Since these did little damage and had little discernible point, the Singapore papers had taken to attributing them to 'the mad bomber of Singapore'. Now, however, Mr Lee Kuan-yew revealed that they were the work of one Masintan Sihombeng, who had been the head of two of Indonesia's 'commercial' organizations, and had recently been arrested. Sihombeng does not seem to have been any more successful as a businessman than as a master-saboteur: his wife told the police that he had been swindled by nearly all the people he had contacted in Singapore.

The hapless Sihombeng was a tragi-comic aspect of Sukarno's neo-imperialism. But there was less room for smiles in the pressures against Sarawak and Sabah, or in the plans for sabotage of water mains, power stations, and other installations revealed by Tunku Abdul Rahman on 18 December 1963.

Nor was there any immediate comfort in the knowledge that Sukarno's fifth columns in Malaysia were unlikely to prove enduring allies. There were, of course, willing recruits to Indonesia's cause among the Indonesians of Sabah, and some among the Malays of Singapore. But the bulk of Sukarno's allies were (overseas) Chinese Communists in Singapore and Sarawak. Some hundreds of Chinese youths, many of them members of Sarawak's Clandestine Communist Organization, had joined the TNKU and TNI guerrillas. But the Chinese who opposed Malaysia in Singapore and Sarawak did so for anti-Malay or Communist reasons that had nothing to do with Sukarno's imperialist ambitions. Indeed they could hardly be unaware that the Chinese were much better treated in Malaya than in Indonesia; or that Indonesian spokesmen continually said that they were against Malaysia because they were afraid the Chinese would gain control of the Federation. Had Indonesia succeeded in 'crushing' Malaysia, the Chinese there would have been the first to suffer.

Sukarno never got as far as agitating against the American bases in the Philippines. He knew the United States was not only much more powerful than Britain in the Far East but more likely to take a long-term view of its need to defend South-East Asia from Communism. Besides, the Filipinos, though they have a longer tradion of nationalism than the Indonesians, are on the whole aware of the value of the American presence on their soil. And Sukarno did not want to take on the Philippines and Malaysia simultaneously.

In January 1964 Mr Robert Kennedy, the American Attorney-General, visited Indonesia and Malaysia on President Johnson's behalf in an effort to bring about a cease-fire in Borneo. In this he was, on paper, successful (though not in reality, for Sukarno refused to withdraw his terrorists from Sarawak and the cease-fire was soon a dead letter). When in Djakarta, Mr Kennedy's party suggested to the Indonesians that the British base in Singapore did not, as the Indonesians argued, infringe Malaysian sovereignty, any more than American bases infringed Philippine sovereignty. Indeed, said the Americans, the United States welcomed the presence of British forces in the area, which they regarded as complementary to that of the U.S. Seventh Fleet. The Indonesians, it is said, refused to be drawn into comparisons which, no doubt, might have found their way back to the Filipinos and offended them.

There could be no doubt of Sukarno's ultimately hostile attitude towards the United States, however. On 24 December 1963 he told a visiting delegation from the South Vietnam Liberation Front that he hoped the Front would soon be victorious so that he could visit a free Saigon. For good measure, he accused the U.S. Seventh Fleet of threatening independent countries in South-East Asia. Since a victory of the Liberation Front would be a defeat for the United States, Sukarno was serving notice that America's enemies are his friends. He rubbed the point in a few weeks later in a public speech, when he turned towards the then American Ambassador, who was present, and said, in English, 'Go to hell with your aid'. The Ambassador, Mr Howard Jones, was generally regarded as the leading American advocate of unconditional support for Sukarno, and was often called 'Merdeka' Jones because he once shouted 'Merdeka!' (freedom) at an Indonesian Independence Day rally.

Now, in August 1966, all the shouting and posturing seemed no more than bitter memories. The agreement between Malaysia and Indonesia provided for free elections in Sabah and Sarawak, to give the peoples of these territories a chance to 'reaffirm ... their previous decision about their status in Malaysia'. This was a sop to Indonesia's and Sukarno's pride, and in his Independence Day speech on the 17th, Sukarno swallowed many past words by declaring his acceptance of the Malaysian-Indonesian agreement because it would enable the people of Sabah and Sarawak to exercise self-determination.

All this was anti-climactic; and indeed there had been an earlier anti-climax – on 9 August 1965, when Mr Lee Kuan-yew took Singapore out of the Malaysian Federation after a long period of worsening relations arising out of money disputes and Malay extremism in Kuala Lumpur. Though Singapore's secession was greeted by Djakarta at the time as an Indonesian victory, it merely underlined a known fact – that it is not easy for Malays and Chinese to live together in harmony. Mr Lee, who understood this, had fought against it, adopting Malay as the official language and in many ways trying to forge a sense of non-communal nationality. Indeed, he didn't give up the attempt, even after secession, and a Malay, Inche Yusuf bin Ishak, became Singapore's first President when the island proclaimed itself a Republic in December 1965. Since then, Singapore and Malaya have gone their separate ways, especially in economic and financial matters. In defence, however, Singapore could not ignore geography, even though, by seceding from the Federation, it had, in effect, opted out of 'confrontation'. True, the island Republic withdrew from the Combined Defence Council with Malaysia at the end of March 1966. But this was followed by public and official assurances that Singapore would continue to consult Malaysia on defence matters.

For all concerned, 'confrontation' had meant serious losses without compensating gains. It had forced Malaya proper into undesirably high defence expenditures and cut Singapore's entrepôt trade by perhaps one-third. Britain and Australia, too, had suffered the expense of sending additional troops to Malaysia and maintaining them. Shortly after the August agreement, British land sea and air forces sent to the area began to be withdrawn; and the Australians of the 4th Battalion, Royal Australian Regiment, left Borneo, where they had replaced Gurkha units on the Indonesian border.

But the biggest losers were undoubtedly the Indonesians. 'Confrontation' completed the ruin inflicted on the State by Sukarno's expansive policies and corrupt administration. When it ended, Indonesia's external debt stood at well over $2,000 million.

In lives lost, the last phase of Sukarno's neo-imperialist* drive had been relatively inexpensive. Indonesia's casualties totalled 1,583, of whom 590 were killed, 222 wounded and 771 captured. Commonwealth military casualties were lighter: 114 killed and 181 wounded. Thirty-six Commonwealth civilians had lost their lives and 53 had been wounded; 4 had been captured. Mercifully, the whole messy and unnecessary affair had fallen short of being a war.

*

It was sadly characteristic of South-East Asia that the end of Confrontation brought Malaysia and Indonesia only temporary relief from political violence. When violence returned, however, late in 1967, it appeared – in both countries – to be controlled from Peking. On 9 February 1968, the Peking press hailed Communist guerrilla victories in Java and Borneo. Three bodies were involved. In Borneo, remnants of the Chinese terrorist bands trained in Indonesia during Confrontation had joined forces with members of the banned Indonesian Communist Party (PKI) to form the PGRS (Sarawak People's Guerrilla Force) and PERAKU (North Borneo People's Force). In West Java, a new underground movement called the TPRI (People's Liberation Army) was in operation.

In Malaysia, the remnants of the Communist bands driven across the Thai border in 1960 went into action again, nominally under the control of the 'Malayan National Liberation League' in Peking, which on 23 February claimed several successes.

*Sukarno's ambitions even extended to Portuguese Timor. A 'United Republic of (Portuguese) Timor' was proclaimed in Djakarta on 14 April 1963 by 'independence fighters'. In itself this event was indeed of little importance to anybody except the Portuguese authorities in eastern Timor and Lisbon. But it merits a mention in a chapter devoted to Sukarno's neo-imperialism.

Nobody could say that Burma is a threat to its neighbours. It is peaceful, neutral, and on reasonably good terms with most other countries. It might therefore seem anomalous to include it among the trouble-spots of South-East Asia. Yet Burma does qualify as a trouble-spot, on several counts. One is internal insecurity: ever since independence, it has been beset by insurrections – both ethnic and ideological – or banditry. Another is its wealth and comparative emptiness: properly developed, it could support several times its present population of anything between twenty-two and twenty-nine million. This could make it tempting for the Chinese giant to the north. Finally, it is a battlefield in the Sino-Soviet dispute.

In some ways, Burma is the most interesting country in South-East Asia. To an even greater degree than the Cambodians or Indonesians, the Burmese have shown themselves determined to clear their own path to the future, rejecting foreign aid and advice. They expelled the American aid mission in 1953 and cancelled five Soviet aid projects in 1959. Cheerful and friendly though the Burman peoples are, they have a tendency towards xenophobia. Behind their barriers of mountain and jungle they want, above all, to be themselves. Lately, indeed, they have gone further still by making it clear that foreign observers are unwelcome. (I myself gave up all hope of visiting

Burma in 1964 after a prolonged wait for a visa. In this, too, the Burmans were behaving like the Cambodians – who had banned 'Anglo-Saxon' journalists – and like the Indonesians, who were keeping British correspondents out.) A further symptom: on 19 April foreigners were forbidden to go to places near Burma's borders with Pakistan, India, China, and Siam.

Clearly, General Ne Win and his Revolutionary Council don't want people to look too closely at what is going on in Burma. This does not make it impossible to find out what is going on, but it does mean that the Burmese leaders' presentation of their own case goes largely by default.

General Ne Win is of Chinese-Burmese parentage. As I mentioned in an earlier chapter, he was one of the thirty 'Thakins' trained in guerrilla warfare by the Japanese. He is now in power for the second time. He first seized power from U Nu and the politicians in September 1958, physically cleaned up Rangoon, virtually eliminated corruption in the civil service and carried out other reforms. Early in 1960, he handed power back to the politicians. Two years later, he decided the latter had shown for the second time that they would never be capable of tackling Burma's problems and he seized power again. This was in March 1962.

General Ne Win sees Burma as a unitary, secular, and socialist State. The socialist part was common ground between him and U Nu; but Ne Win wants to build socialism more efficiently than U Nu seemed likely to do it, with his easy-going nature, parliamentary methods, and tolerance of corruption. Ne Win's differences with U Nu over the nature of the Burmese State were more fundamental.

In his campaign for the general elections of February 1960, which signalled Burma's return to constitutional life after Ne Win's first taste of power, U Nu had promised the Mon and Arakanese minorities the right to form autonomous States within the Union. There were already other such States – Shan and Kayah, for instance – but Ne Win, a centralist, had no liking for them and probably felt that the more there were the greater would be the danger to Burma's already precarious unity. The last straw that provoked the general to seize power a second time was an even more direct threat to central rule – a demand from the Shans for the dissolution of the Union and its replacement by a federal system.

General Ne Win's other major difference with U Nu concerned religion. In his election campaign, U Nu had promised to make Buddhism the established religion – a proposal that won him the support of the influential Buddhist monks, but was potentially yet another blow to Burma's unity in that it was bound, if implemented, to alienate non-Buddhist communities, such as the Arakanese Moslems and the Karen Christians.

In the event, U Nu took no action on his promises to the minority peoples, but he did make Buddhism the State religion. One of the first things Ne Win did on seizing power for the second time was to dissolve the five State Councils, which dealt with Shan, Kachin, Karen, Kayah, and Chin affairs. These he replaced with new State Supreme Councils, all headed by men supporting the existing unitary State. Two months later, on 1 May 1962, the Revolutionary Council's 'Burmese Socialism' programme was published. The entry under 'Religion' read: 'The Revolutionary Council recognizes the right of everyone freely to profess and practise his religion.' On Burma's national groups, the programme had this to say:

In striving towards the fraternity aud unity of all the races of the Union, we shall be guided by what General Aung San, our national leader, said at the AFPFL conference held at the Shwe Dagon Pagoda on 20 January 1946: 'A nation is a collective term applied to a people, irrespective of their ethnic origin, living in close contact with one another and having common interests and sharing joys and sorrows together for such historic periods as to have acquired a sense of oneness. Though race, religion, and language are important factors, it is their traditional desire and will to live in unity through weal and woe that binds a people together and makes them a nation.' We, the peoples of the Union of Burma, shall nurture a new patriotism inspired by the words of General Aung San.

This time, Ne Win's disillusionment with democracy was complete and he didn't promise to hand power back to the politicians. Indeed, the Army rounded up U Nu and other politicians and placed them under house arrest, where they remained for years. For good measure, he had the opposition leaders, headed by U Ba Swe, arrested in August 1963.

Insurgency had again become a formidable problem when General Ne Win took over. The biggest of the 'ethnic' rebel groups was the Karen National Defence Organization (KNDO) with about 6,000 men under arms. The Shan State Independence Army and the Shan State Liberation Front together mustered between 3,000 and 5,000. Then there was the Kachin Independence Army, with perhaps 1,000 men. These figures are, of course, approximations to the truth. Many of the rebels had acquired a taste for fighting and pillage and fought on because they liked it rather than for any precise aims. Both the Karens and the Kachins, however, wanted independence – that is, the right to secede from the Union of Burma. The Shans would have settled for a federal State, with equal rights and perpetual right of secession, that is, independence whenever they might feel like it. In addition to the ethnic rebels, there were two Communist insurgent groups: the Trotskyist Red Flags, about 500 in number, led by Thakin Soe; and the White Flags of the Burma Communist Party (BCP), numbering about 1,000. Originally the White Flags had represented the orthodox Moscow line, as distinct from the Trotskyism of the Red Flags. But, late in 1962, the Moscow-line leader of the BCP, Thakin Than Tun, was ousted by a Peking-line man, H. N. Ghoshal. This added another complication to the already complex pattern of challenges to Ne Win's authority.

General Ne Win made a bold, but in the end unavailing, bid to end insurgency by negotiation. On 1 April 1963 he offered a general amnesty. This persuaded a few rebels to come back to civilian life, but not enough of them to make much difference. In June he invited all underground groups to come to Rangoon for unconditional peace talks. Most of them turned up: the Red Flags, the White Flags, the Kachins, and the Karens. The main talks lasted from August to November, and nearly all were broken off by one side or another, the rebels returning to their hills or jungles. In the end only the right-wing Karens remained (the left wing, having made common cause with the White Flags, followed them back into dissidence); and on 13 March 1964 a cease-fire agreement with the non-Communist Karens was announced. Perhaps the most striking outcome of the breakdown of the talks with the Communists was the arrest, between 15 and 17 November 1963, of several hundred Communists or sympathizers. General Ne Win was showing that he would no more brook opposition from the anti-parliamentary left than from the democratic politicians.

This brings me back to the Communist challenge. The Red Flags and White Flags (BCP), being illegal, were known as the 'underground' Communists. But there were 'legal' Communists too, and these were known as the 'above-ground' Communists. For some years, there were two above-ground groups: the Burma Workers' Party and the People's Comrade Party. In 1962, they merged to form the United Workers' Party, under the leadership of U Chit Maung. Now just as the illegal BCP had gone over to Peking, ideologically, so the United Workers' Party was committed to the Moscow line.

In practical terms, this split had a direct bearing on tactics. Though there is no evidence that the Chinese People's Republic has ever given material aid of any significance to the White Flags, Peking probably gave the orders during the abortive peace talks. At any rate several leaders of the BCP were in Peking when Ne Win's negotiating proposals were announced, and the Chinese authorities arranged the flight to Rangoon. Just before the collapse of the talks, the Burmese security services had intercepted and decoded messages from the BCP leaders to the negotiators which made it clear that these were trying to gain time, persuade Ne Win to endorse a Communist administration in the White Flag rebel areas, and, at the right moment, 'intensify the struggle' against his 'fascist' régime.

The Moscow-leaning United Workers' Party, in contrast, was under orders to infiltrate into Ne Win's administration and try to steer it in a Marxist-Leninist direction. To this end, a number of the above-ground Communists resigned from the United Workers' Party to take important jobs near the centre of power. One of them was U Ba Nyein, who became a director of the Union Bank of Burma and the government's financial adviser. Another was Thakin Tin Mya, who became Ne Win's political adviser. The arrests of November 1963 were, no doubt, a stunning blow to the hopes of the above-ground Communists. But these two men, and others, still had the general's ear.

Ne Win, who had founded the Socialist Programme Party to implement the Revolutionary Council's policy, seemed determined, nevertheless, to steer an independent course. The arrests were one sign of this; and on 28 March 1964 he took the logical next step of banning all political parties but his own. The military and socialist dictatorship was complete.

It is of course too early to give a definitive verdict on Ne Win's régime. But at the risk of being unfair, an interim appraisal may be attempted. One thing is clear enough: the character of the régime is in closer harmony with Burma's despotic past than with the brave democratic hopes aroused by U Nu's fumbling but well-meant efforts. The fundamental liberties have gone and Burma is a near-totalitarian State. Many injustices have been committed. Local business men, guiltless of crime, have not only had their assets expropriated without compensation but have been stripped of all their possessions and turned out into the street with only the clothes on their backs.

With the partial exception of the right-wing Karens, the Revolutionary Council has failed to bring peace to the minority areas. Indeed hatred of Burmese central rule is more bitter than ever. Meanwhile, Burmese socialism proceeds apace. On 23 February 1963, at 1 p.m., tanks surrounded all banks in Rangoon and heavily-armed troops forced the managers to hand over the keys of the vaults. Now all such institutions are called People's Banks. All trade, including internal distribution of foodstuffs, has been nationalized. As a result, commerce is at a standstill and the new military managers of the People's Banks have little work to do. Confiscatory taxes have been imposed (the tax on cars, of instance, was raised by *3,000 per cent* at the beginning of 1964).

It could not be said, five years after the 1962 coup, that these measures were solving Burma's economic problems. Farmers owed the State about £37·5 million in loans they were unable to repay. Unemployment reached 1,800,000 in 1966 and went on rising. In real terms, the income *per capita* was probably 15 per cent below the pre-war level. Meanwhile, Burma has taken to trading in gold, running down its sterling balances to such a low level that on 17 October 1966, on Britain's suggestion, Burma withdrew from the sterling area.

This, too, was in line with the régime's xenophobia; and at the end of the year a further sign came with the expulsion of Christian missionaries. Earlier, foreign news agencies and the Rockefeller, Ford and Asia Foundations had been expelled. Time only will tell whether General Ne Win will live up to the remark he once made: 'Let us get the country in order first and then I hope it will be thrown open as before'. Meanwhile, a welcome sign of relaxation was the release, on 27 October 1966 of the former AFPFL leaders, U Nu and U Ba Swe, followed, in February 1967, by the release of 50 other detainees.

Where is it all leading? I have little doubt that Ne Win, however rough his methods, is fundamentally a patriotic Burman, who believes socialism is best for his country and wants the Burmans to find their own way to it. In 1967, he showed convincingly that he is always ready to assert Burma's independence when he finds it threatened by a bigger power. The surest sign of this was the departure in November of the 500 technicians who had been working in Burma on projects under a massive Chinese aid programme since 1961. Ne Win's suspicions had been aroused when it was clear that the Chinese were mainly interested in building strategic bridges that could have been used to bring Chinese troops into Burma. A major White Flag campaign of terrorism, backed by Peking, came next; and Ne Win expelled the New China News Agency correspondent, rounded up 200 Peking sympathizers and mobilized Burma's propaganda resources to discredit China.

As 1967 drew to a close, insecurity was as bad as ever, with perhaps 30 per cent of the country under insurgent control. Geography is indeed against Burma's search for identity and independence.

Part Five TODAY AND TOMORROW

Chapter One WESTERN INTERESTS

The West as a whole has a general interest in the peace and prosperity of South-East Asia; and therefore in opposing the aggressive manifestations of both Communism and nationalism. Should the West go further and busy itself with a country's ruling ideology? The answer must surely be conditioned by the character of the ideology. If it is hostile to the West, or damaging to Western interests, including investments and trade, then Western nations can hardly pretend that a country's ideology is of no interest to them. In all cases the advent of Communism affects investments and trade; usually it affects the strategic balance of power as well (as in Cuba), though there are exceptions: nobody could say that Tito's Jugoslavia, for all its Communist ideology, was much of a threat to world peace. Nationalism can also be damaging to Western interests, as the Dutch and British have discovered in Indonesia.

The West is far from united in its attitude to such questions, or to South-East Asia as a regional problem. The French have made it clear that they would be happier if Indo-China were 'neutral', with at least one Communist government still in power there (in North Vietnam) than if American forces stayed there indefinitely. Since this attitude, which has led the French to boycott SEATO, reflects General de Gaulle's anti-Anglo-Saxon obsession and his discounting of 'communism' as a factor in international relations, it must be regarded as idiosyn-cratic. By this, I do not mean that the French attitude is unimportant; but that de Gaulle's foreign policies will not necessarily be adopted by successor governments.

The British attitude is more complex. It is conditioned, among other things, by the permanent crisis of the Sterling Area and the desire of the Macmillan and Wilson governments to 'go into Europe'. These factors have encouraged the view that British defence commitments east of Suez are not only unnecessary but even undesirable, on both political and econo-mic grounds. As anybody knows who has read the speeches of the Conservative spokesman on defence, Mr Enoch Powell, this is a view that is by no means confined to the Labour Party, in power since 1964.

A long period of ambiguity in official policy on withdrawal east of Suez was ended abruptly in the wake of Britain's devaluation crisis towards the end of 1967. On 10 January 1968, the Prime Minister, Mr Wilson, announced that British forces would be withdrawn from the Far East (except Hong Kong) by the end of 1971 – and not, as had been foreshadowed, by the mid-1970s. The news was greeted with consternation in the countries most closely affected by it. Mr Gorton, the Australian Prime Minister, expressed regret; the Malaysian government its grave disappointment; and the United States 'regret'. The strongest opposition came from Mr Lee Kuan-yew of Singapore, who flew to London in a vain attempt to persuade Mr Wilson to change his mind.

Although I have long been convinced of the need for Britain to join Europe, I believe the policy of abandonment east of Suez to be profoundly mistaken. The argument that it is necessary for financial reasons does not hold water, for there are other and better ways of solving Britain's economic ills: for instance, by modernizing its technology and improving productivity; by reducing imports; and by exploring far more fully than has been done hitherto the chances of creating a new inter-national currency to finance world trade. Britain, in fact, can afford to stay east of Suez as well as play its full part in Europe.

The argument that commitments east of Suez are politically incompatible, in the long run, with Britain's European vocation seems to me to be equally indefensible. Or rather, it is true only in the restricted sense that de Gaulle used the argument to support his veto on British entry into the European Economic Community. True, de Gaulle did not actually say that Britain must withdraw east of Suez. But this was implicit in all his innuendoes about England being an 'island', Britain's special relations with the United States, the 'Anglo-Saxons', the need for England to prove itself 'European', and so forth. If entry into Europe can be secured only by appeasing de Gaulle – by severing the special links with the United States, accepting France's leadership in European defence and abandoning global responsibilities – then the price is too high.

Britain is, in fact, stronger and richer than ever in its history; and neither its relative decline – relatively to America and Russia – nor its shedding of a vast empire, need blind one to this.

More than most peoples, the British must take a global view of defence and strategy; 'little England' is a candidate for extinction. The prevalence of the contrary view has led to a rapid but largely unnecessary decline in Britain's influence throughout South-East Asia and the Far East. In fact, the contribution Britain can make to peace and stability in one of the most troubled areas of the world is still enormous. It is a contribution that cannot be measured in manpower and 'hardware' alone, though both were brilliantly effective in containing Indonesia's 'confrontation'. More important still are accumulated knowledge and expertise, and acceptability to local populations. Once such assets are thrown away, they can never be regained. As Mr McNamara, the American Defence Secretary, said on 11 April 1967, the continued presence of British forces in the Middle and Far East 'contributes significantly to peace-keeping and security'. At a time when – largely through the creation and presence of NATO – the Soviet threat in Europe has receded, it makes no sense at all to argue that Britain should abandon its contribution to peace-keeping in a truly threatened area like South-East Asia.

Against such reasons of wider and enlightened self-interest, economic considerations carry relatively little weight. Economically, Britain has no 'vital' interests in South-East Asia. True, there are sizeable investments in Malaysia, Brunei and Singapore; and the British investments in Indonesia were valued at £400 million in the late 1950s, before Sukarno started grabbing them. But Britain would be little affected by the loss of its South-East Asian capital though individual companies would feel the pinch.

Apart from reasons of enlightened self-interest, the British are, in fact, involved in South-East Asia's troubles through a number of precise commitments. The most important of these is the commitment to defend Malaysia under the London Agreement of 8 July 1963. Singapore's subsequent withdrawal from Malaysia left a question-mark over the island's defence, but Britain has promised to stay as long as she is welcome; in the meantime, Singapore is taking steps to improve its own defence capability. A broader commitment to the area as a whole arises from Britain's membership of SEATO, inconvenient though it may have become to pay more than lip service to it.

To these may be added the unwritten obligations assumed by the British Foreign Secretary as co-chairman (with the Soviet Foreign Minister) of the two Geneva conferences – on Indo-China in 1954, and on Laos in 1961–2. What this really means is that any complaints about the way the agreements are being implemented, and any proposals relating to them, are normally addressed in the first instance to Britain and Russia. Since neither of the Geneva settlements has stood the test of time, however, the co-chairman's role has tended to become invidious; although it is politically useful to Harold Wilson to keep the fractious left wing of his party quiet by emphasizing the mediatory possibilities open to Britain as co-chairman of the Geneva conferences. On any sane reading of national interest and allied solidarity, however, the commitments to SEATO and Malaysia are more important than the residual utility of the co-chairmanship. Some consolation was to be drawn, however, from a clear pledge made in the House of Commons on 5 March 1968, by the Conservative Opposition leader, Mr Heath, that a Conservative government would send British forces back 'east of Suez' if the countries concerned agreed.

As Britain's reluctance to assume its responsibilities in South-East Asia has grown, so have Australia and New Zealand been increasingly forced to assume theirs. Until the Second World War shattered cosy traditions, Australians and New Zealanders depended unquestioningly on Imperial Britain for their defence. The sinking of the *Prince of Wales* and the *Repulse* and the fall of Singapore to the Japanese in 1942 made them turn to America for the protection Britain could no longer give. And the altered circumstances of Pacific strategy were reflected in the Australia, New Zealand and United States Treaty (ANZUS) of 1951.

Geographically, Australia and New Zealand are 'white' extensions of South-East Asia. Both are threatened, but particularly the former by regional crises in a way Britain is not. For Australia, in particular, 'confrontation' was an unnerving time. And now that Indonesia has ceased to be an immediate danger, both countries are still, and increasingly involved in the much larger confrontation in Vietnam. That this involvement makes sense, not merely to armchair strategists but to those most closely concerned – the Australian and New Zealand voters – has been proved at the polls. In an election fought largely on the issue of military involvement in Vietnam, the late Harold Holt's Liberal-Country coalition was returned to power with a greatly increased majority in November 1966. Simultaneously, and with similar issues involved, Mr Holyoake's National Party was returned to power in New Zealand, though with a net loss of one seat. Since then, Australia's forces in Vietnam have been increased by 2,400 men to about 8,000. (New Zealand has 540 men and an artillery battery serving in South Vietnam.) In January 1967, both Mr Holt and Mr Holyoake were hosts to the Prime Minister of South Vietnam, Air-Vice-Marshal Nguyen Cao Ky.

In the broadest sense, of course, the security of South-East Asia continues to depend on the presence of the American Seventh Fleet and the willingness of the United States to carry such burdens as the one already being carried in Vietnam. But other countries' contributions are not neglible, if only because they demonstrate better than any words, a recognition of interests and willingness to defend them.

Chapter Two SUKARNO'S LEGACY

To an overwhelming extent, the Indonesian problem was Sukarno's personal responsibility. He had built around him a fantastic edifice of pleasure, corruption and make-believe. Inflated dreams of grandeur were based on a foundation of inflated currency. It became highly profitable to be a crony of the President's and uncomfortable or dangerous to notice that the head of the ramshackle empire had no clothes on. Exile, gaol or poverty was the choice open to dissenters.

As theatre, Sukarno's performance was superb; as a contribution to political theory, it was essentially impermanent. The wonder was that it lasted so long, and took in so many people. For millions of Indonesians, 'Bung' Karno's empty speeches blinded them to the horrid reality of deepening poverty and even, at times, starvation. Outside Indonesia, many accepted at face value his claim to the leadership of the 'new emerging forces' – typically expressed in the slogan word Nefo.

In terms of significance and power, the dream dissolved on 12 March 1967, when the Indonesian People's Consultative Congress unanimously resolved to revoke Sukarno's mandate as President. All powers granted to him under the 1945 Constitution were withdrawn, and another unanimous resolution stripped him of his grandest honorific title, 'Great Leader of the Indonesian Revolution'. General Suharto – a calm, quiet, skilful officer who had been presiding over the decline in Sukarno's fortunes – was appointed Acting President until the general elections could be held.

It had taken Suharto 15 months to depose Sukarno, and his success of 12 March was the reward of an astute and patient strategy. He had needed all his patience and astuteness, for Sukarno had fought every inch of the downward way, feinting and weaving with such skill that it often looked to the outside world as though he might yet emerge the victor.

The early months of the prolonged singular combat between Suharto and Sukarno went by against the background of one of the greatest blood-baths of modern times – the massacre of perhaps half a million Indonesians, loosely described as 'communists' by their fellow countrymen. Indeed the fall of Sukarno was inextricably linked with the near-extinction of Indonesia's powerful Communist Party, the PKI.

It was the second time in one generation that the PKI had been annihilated. In 1948, after the abortive Madiun uprising, the party was crushed and its leadership dead or discredited. Yet in 1965, when the first edition of this book appeared, the PKI had about 3 million members and a mass following among PKI-controlled peasants', workers', youth and women's organizations. The party's astonishing recovery, after the slaughter of 1948, was the work of an able young leader, Dipa Nusantara Aidit, who was in his late twenties when he gained control of it as Secretary-General in 1953. The crushing of the 1958 rebellion – in which the PKI's arch-enemies, the Socialist and Masjumi (modern Moslem) parties were implicated – further enhanced its relative power. The slogan NASAKOM (nationalists, religious people and Communists), officially adopted in 1960 as part of President Sukarno's 'guided democracy', recognized the PKI as one of the three main forces in Indonesian politics. In fact, however, the three forces that counted were the Army, the PKI and Sukarno, who kept himself in power largely by playing off the soldiers against the Communists. Indeed, having crushed the politicians, he clearly decided that a strong PKI was essential to his balancing act. After several attempts to bring the PKI into his cabinet in the face of strong Army resistance,

Sukarno succeeded on 27 August 1964, when Aidit's second deputy, Njoto, was appointed Minister attached to the Presidium.

Now there seemed to be no stopping Aidit, whose luck apparently matched his skill. Safe, as he thought, under the President's protective mantle, he worked at two levels simultaneously. From below, his followers infiltrated the armed forces, both in the ranks and at the junior officer level, where their work was made easy by the propaganda diet of NASAKOM constantly being fed into the officers' corps. Officially, the line that flowed down from President Sukarno was that there were no longer Communists and non-Communists in Indonesia: everybody was 'NASAKOM'. This blurring of dividing lines played into Aidit's hands. While the PKI's infiltration went on, Communist-led mobs seized foreign enterprises, forcing the State to nationalize them. From above, meanwhile, the Communists in the government constantly criticized Djakarta's economic policies on the ground that they were insufficiently socialistic. They were careful, however, to praise Sukarno himself; and this manoeuvred the President into adopting more and more of their programme.

In 1965, Aidit decided to force the pace. In January, he had achieved a further success when the President banned the PKI's main ideological rival, the Murba (Proletariat) Party, which advocated national communism without international communist links. In March, he had his first setback, when the Communists failed to spark off a mutiny in the Navy. During the next two months, however, a number of high-ranking anti-Communist police officers were removed after the PKI had criticized them.

By mid-1965, both sides – the Army and the PKI – were preparing for a showdown. Despite communist infiltration at the lower and middle levels, the higher Army officers had remained determinedly anti-Communist. They heard with alarm of Communist plans for an armed force of their own. At first the PKI had called for a people's Militia of armed peasants under Communist control. Under Army pressure, Sukarno turned this request down, but he showed signs of favouring an alternative proposal for a 'Fifth Force' (in addition to the Army, Navy, Air Force and Police) of armed workers under Communist leadership.

The Army's dilemma was that it was powerful enough to crush the PKI but feared to do so while Sukarno was in power; while every month that passed increased the Communists' relative power. The PKI, on its side, wanted to delay the showdown as long as possible. Suddenly, however, events forced Aidit's hand.

For years, Sukarno had suffered from kidney trouble: it was said that one of his kidneys had ceased to function and the other was deteriorating fast. A Chinese doctor, sent from Peking at the President's request, examined him late in July and decided that Sukarno could not live much longer. By passing the news on to the PKI, he provided the spark that fired the Indonesian tinder-box. For the PKI now decided to speed up its plans for a take-over. From subsequent events and the statements of captured plotters, it is known that at the first sign of Sukarno's physical collapse, all the leading anti-Communist generals and politicians were to be assassinated. An outwardly non-Communist Revolutionary Council would take over; and the Communists would come into the open at a later stage.

On the evening of 30 September, Sukarno collapsed while addressing a meeting in Djakarta stadium. He was carried off the platform, and Aidit, who was in the audience, slipped away. Aidit therefore did not learn, until it was too late, that the President's collapse was only temporary, for Sukarno later returned to the rostrum and resumed his speech. Rumours that the President had died had spread like wildfire, and reached the man who had been selected as the PKI's revolutionary instrument, Lieutenant-Colonel Untung, commander of the Presidential Guard. Immediately, and prematurely, the Communist plan was put into action. Squads of his troops left the Palace grounds with orders to kidnap the leading eight generals and take them to Halim air base, 15 miles from Djakarta's town centre.

In the event, six only of the generals were kidnapped: all were murdered after bestial tortures. The other two escaped, and this brought about the PKI's downfall.

One of the two was General Abdul Haris Nasution: his small daughter was killed by his kidnappers, but he himself escaped with a wound. The other was Major-General Suharto, who was not at home when the murderers called. Nasution – then Defence Minister – was Indonesia's best-known soldier, and for a long time the Americans had put great store on him as a potential 'saviour' of Indonesia, both from Communism and from Sukarno. In earlier editions of this book, I discounted this theory, on the ground that Nasution's past history showed that he lacked the nerve to rid Indonesia of Sukarno. The fact that he was wounded in the 30 September coup, however, gave Suharto his opportunity. At the time, he was hardly known outside Army circles. But stepping into the shoes of the murdered Army Chief of Staff, General Jani, Suharto soon showed that he had the qualities Nasution lacked: nerve, caution and political skill.

Was President Sukarno a party to the 30 September plot? Probably not, in the fullest sense, since he could hardly have joined a movement to set up a Communist administration after his own death. On the other hand, he seems to have accepted the PKI's argument that a coup would be needed, at some time, to forestall an alleged plot by the Army generals, with the support of the American Central Intelligence Agency, to seize power. Untung, finding the President was still alive, kidnapped him and took him to Halim air base, where the generals had been taken before their murder, and where the Air Force Commander, General Omar Dani, was to take over on behalf of the plotters.

There is no space here to describe in detail the 30 September coup and its consequences.* A bare outline must suffice. The most horrific consequence was the mass slaughter of Communists or sympathizers in Java, Sumatra, Bali and other islands. The best estimate is that between 300,000 and 500,000 people were butchered in the five months from October 1965 to February 1966. The first casualties resulted from clashes between the Army and armed supporters of the PKI. But the massacres that followed were instigated by fanatical Moslems of the

* For a full account, see Tarzie Vittachi's *The Fall of Sukarno* (Mayflower Books, London, 1967).

Nahdatul Ulama (religious teachers) party in a 'holy war' against Communist atheism.

The coup itself swiftly collapsed. Untung had issued a communiqué in the name of a Revolutionary Council (on which Sukarno's name did not appear), but was captured, tried and sentenced to death. Aidit, the communist leader, was found in hiding and shot out of hand by the Army; so was Njoto, who had been the PKI's first Minister.

One by one Sukarno's closest associates were brought to trial in the autumn of 1966. The most unpopular was Dr Subandrio, the former Foreign Minister, who had also been head of the Central Intelligence Bureau. He was found guilty of embezzling $500,000 and complicity in the Communist plot, and sentenced to death. The former Minister of Central Banking, Jusuf Muda Dalam, was also sentenced to death, for embezzling $10 million and lavishing illegal gifts on private companies and on his wives and mistresses. Death was likewise the sentence on Air Force General Omar Dani.

Before the political trials, and while the massacres were in progress, Sukarno and Subandrio had made what was nearly a successful attempt at a come-back. On 21 February 1966, the President announced a new version of his NASAKOM cabinet, to include Subandrio and PKI representatives, together with Suharto, but excluding Nasution. The announcement touched off widespread anti-Sukarno student demonstrations and riots, in the course of which the Foreign Ministry – Subandrio's headquarters – was wrecked. The riots continued, and Suharto was able to persuade Sukarno, on the night of 11-12 March, to hand over all executive power to him.

Suharto thereupon formed his own cabinet with two 'super-Ministers' to assist him. Adam Malik, a former leader of the banned Murba party, became Foreign Minister, with nine related Ministries under him; and the able and honest Sultan of Jogjakarta, Hamenghu Buwono IX, a former Defence Minister, was put in charge of finance and economics, also with nine subsidiary Ministries. A week later, Subandrio and fourteen other former Ministers were placed under 'protective custody' and Sukarno was confined to his two Palaces in Djakarta and

Bogor, with an Army helicopter to take him from one to the other but nowhere else.

Throughout the prolonged crisis, Suharto gently resisted the impatient counsels of his friends, who wished him either to exile Sukarno or bring him to trial. He preferred to whittle the President's powers away, and discredit him. On 5 July 1966, the People's Consultative Congress deprived Sukarno of his title of Life President; on 13 February 1967, the Supreme Court called for Sukarno's trial for alleged treason, corruption and embezzlement; and on 22 February, Sukarno signed away all his remaining powers to Suharto, while retaining the title of President. As we have seen, Suharto completed his victory on 12 March, when he was appointed Acting President.

*

The legacy of Sukarno's 21 years of power was a heavy one. The only thing that can be said in his favour is that he used his charismatic appeal to unite the diverse peoples of the great archipelago and give them a sense of Indonesian nationhood, and a common language. Against must be set the discrediting of public service and the press, the poisoning of public opinion, the bankruptcy of the State, the progressive ruin of the economy and the costly futility of his foreign policy. His successors have worked with deliberate speed to undo the damage. As we have seen (Part Four, Chapter Four), they have ended the 'confrontation' with Malaysia, so that, once again, Indonesia is a good neighbour in South-East Asia. The Peking–Djakarta Axis, which developed hand in hand with 'confrontation' and the rise of the PKI, is dead and unlikely to be revived in the near future. Indeed, in September 1967, Indonesia suspended trade relations with Peking; a month later, diplomatic relations were suspended too. Sukarno had taken Indonesia out of the United Nations and the International Monetary Fund; Suharto, Malik and the Sultan renewed its membership of both bodies. Sukarno had tried to launch a grouping – Maphilindo – which Indonesia would have dominated. In August 1967 Suharto and his colleagues brought Indonesia into a wider and more hopeful gathering known as the Association of South-East Asian Nations (ASEAN), in partnership with Malaysia, Singapore, Thailand and the Philippines. (The new group is to absorb an older one, ASA, which linked Thailand with the Philippines and Malaysia.)

The undoing of Sukarno's foreign policy was an essential prelude to tackling the appalling mess left by Sukarno's financial and economic irresponsibility; for only when international confidence in Indonesia had been restored would foreign credits be made available. A Herculean task faced Sukarno's successors. During the last few years of his rule, prices had risen at least 800-fold, and Indonesia's foreign debts had reached $2·5 *billion* – about $1,000 million of which was owed to the Soviet Union, largely for arms and equipment. Emergency aid came in September 1966 from the 'Tokyo club' – Japan and some of Indonesia's other creditors, including the United States, Australia, Britain, Germany and India. In November, Russia agreed to reschedule debt payments over thirteen years; and in December, the Tokyo Club also granted easy repayment terms. But it will be years before Indonesia is out of the red; and perhaps more years before its severely wounded economy resumes its forward march.

Chapter Three THE MODERNIZERS

The outsider can do less about some South-East Asian problems than about others. It is useful to distinguish between these problems. Broadly speaking, outsiders can do little about internal problems, but are under less restraint where external problems are concerned.

One may or may not think General Ne Win's nationalization of Burma's retail trade was misguided, approve or disapprove of Indonesia's treatment of the Indonesian Chinese minority; but there is little an outsider can do about either. It is, however, quite a different matter when one government starts interfering with another and encroaching on its territory, especially when a Western Power is under an obligation to defend the victim. This was the case with both South Vietnam and Malaysia. The Americans cannot abandon the Vietnamese, nor could the British leave the Malaysians defenceless before Sukarno's threats. There is no need to be afraid of ritual curse-words, such as 'imperialism' or 'neo-colonialism', which ill fit Powers that have withdrawn from their colonial possessions in South-East Asia. The imperialist boot, as I have tried to show, is on the other foot.

Just as one should distinguish between problems, so one should distinguish between friendly or sensible governments on the one hand, and hostile or misguided ones on the other. This is particularly relevant in the case of economic or financial aid programmes. One may not be able to interfere in the running of another country's affairs (at least not for long) but one is under no obligation to prop up governments whose approach to financial matters is irresponsible and whose conduct of foreign affairs is dangerous. Once again the most exquisite example of both was Sukarno's Indonesia. Yet the British and American governments went on giving aid to Indonesia long after it was apparent both that it would be wasted and that it would bring no return in good will. The predictable outcome was a gigantic financial mess from which, as we have seen, Japan and various western countries – and even the Soviet Union, whose massive deliveries of arms were a major cause of both unrest and financial instability – are trying to extricate General Suharto and his Government.

By and large, indeed, governments that demonstrate their willingness to tackle their countries' real problems and leave others in peace should get priority in Western aid programmes.

But aid cannot be imposed on an unwilling recipient: Prince Sihanouk's Cambodia, for instance, though it tackles its own problems and leaves its neighbours in peace, doesn't want American aid.

The principle of helping one's friends is nevertheless a sound guide to action. As I have said, even South-East Asia's Western-minded leaders are not 'pro-Western' in the sense in which that term is used in Western newspapers. In a broad sense, however, they are men – either leaders or potential leaders – who are modern-minded and aware of the sterility of Communism and backward-looking traditions. To the extent that politicians can be regarded as the friends of other politicians, these men are friends.

There are, alas, remarkably few of them. Among those actu-ally in power one must list the leaders of Malaysia and Singapore, Tunku Abdul Rahman and Mr Lee. The Tunku is getting on in years and talks of retiring. His deputy and probable successor, Tun Abdul Razak bin Hussein – quieter by tempera-ment than the Tunku but a prodigious worker – is also a 'modernizer', as his work for rural development in Malaya has proved. Lee Kuan-yew – one of the most remarkable personalities of South-East Asia – has an important part to play in the area, even though his Chinese origin limits the possibilities open to him.

President Marcos and the other Filipino politicians must also be regarded as friends, even though the Philippine claim to North Borneo involved the Philippines, to some extent, on Indonesia's side in opposing Malaysia. Understandably, the Filipinos are anxious, these days, to demonstrate that they are Asians and not, as some fellow-Asians seemed to assume, Americans in disguise. But the important thing is that, for all the tales of corruption in Manila, Western ideas of freedom flourish in the Philippines. Although both Malaysia and the Philippines remain under threat from Communist parties, neither – at the time of writing – was threatened by a reversion to oriental despotism.

Friends who are out of power are harder to help. But they should not be forgotten. The able, modern-minded men who rebelled against the corruption and inefficiency of Sukarno's régime in 1958 – men like Dr Sumitro, the former Finance Minister, and Dr Sjafruddin, the former Governor of the Bank of Indonesia – may yet play a part in the reconstruction of their country's shattered economy. The honest and intelligent Sultan of Jogjakarta, a former Defence Minister who was in the political wilderness for years, is back at the centre as Suharto's economic overlord. The fearless and talented journalist and novelist, Mochtar Lubis, is at work again after nine years in Sukarno's gaols. It is men like these who may rescue Indonesia from its discreditable chaos.

It will be seen that the range of choices open to the United States and other Western countries is very narrow. But if there are no ready-made solutions, the West can at least stick to its commitments and help its friends. In the long run, this will be better than turning our backs on South-East Asia.

At the beginning of 1965, the Viet Cong appeared to be within sight of victory in South Vietnam. The overthrow and murder of President Ngo Dinh Diem on 1 November 1963 had left a dangerous power vacuum, which short-lived military régimes had failed to fill satisfactorily. The Americans, though their presence had become essential to the survival of any anti-Communist or even anti-neutralist government in Saigon, were quite powerless to prevent a bewildering succession of *coups d'état*, although such instability seriously handicapped the prosecution of the war.

On the ground, the Viet Cong had grown fast in strength, firepower and boldness. With about 35,000 'regulars' and perhaps 80,000 part-timers, the Communist army kept the initiative, attacking at will, melting when attacked. This compact and formidable foe seemed more than a match for the more numerous and better equipped Vietnamese army, even with the support of a mounting number of Americans. The South Vietnamese army, on the other hand, was handicapped by administrative and garrison duties in the towns and cities. The Viet Cong, living off the land, had a less unwieldy and therefore more mobile army.

In retrospect, it seems probable that had the Lao Dong Party decided to offer negotiations at this critical stage, it might have gained enough of its fundamental aims to make sure of gaining the rest in due course. But the Vietnamese Communists were not – and are still not – interested in half or two-thirds of the cake; they wanted the lot. On 7 February 1965, the Communist guerrillas struck at the American airfield and billet area at Pleiku in the central highlands, killing or wounding 70 Americans and destroying 17 helicopters and three transport planes. That afternoon, American and South Vietnamese planes retaliated against North Vietnamese targets. It can now be seen that 7 February 1965 was a decisive date, marking a turning point in the war. The escalation that has alarmed so much of the world began that day; and it was the Viet Cong who began it.

What made the Vietnamese Communists do it? Although the answers are bound to be speculative, some attempt must be made to find them. The main reason was undoubtedly the dominant position within the North Vietnamese ruling party held by the First Secretary, Le Duan, founder of the National Liberation Front and the advocate of war to the bitter end. Another reason may be found in the circumstances prevailing within the Communist world at that time. The struggle between Moscow and Peking for control of the world's Communist parties was at its height and the Russians were trying to attract as many parties as possible to Moscow for a showdown conference. The Lao Dong party, by then deeply under Chinese influence, was threatening to boycott the proposed conference. The Russians, however, knew that they were in a position to offer North Vietnam modern military equipment, whereas the Chinese were not. They probably reasoned that by playing this trump card, they could do several things at once – win back the allegiance of the Lao Dong Party, improve their prestige within the international Communist movement at China's expense, and enhance their chances of playing a dominant role in a future peace conference.

On 26 November 1964, the Russians pledged all necessary help to North Vietnam; and early in February, the new Soviet Premier, Kosygin, headed a powerful Soviet delegation in Hanoi talks.

It was at this stage, while the Russians were in Hanoi, that the Viet Cong struck at the Americans; and this timing gives a clue to the reasoning of the North Vietnamese Communists in ordering them to strike. Doubtless, with the war faction in the ascendant, they aimed at forcing the Russians to give them unlimited help against the Americans. Le Duan may well have seen this as a golden opportunity to counter any Soviet suggestions for a peace conference; he would have had support from Ho Chi Minh, always ready to grasp the chance of playing off Moscow against Peking. At that time, it is fair to assume that the entire Lao Dong leadership – intoxicated by their successes in 'revolutionary' war, aware of declining morale in South Vietnam, and uncritically receptive to China's view of America as a 'paper tiger' – discounted the possibility of massive intervention from America. Military victory in the South now seemed feasible.

It is clear that the Russians were not told in advance of the Viet Cong attacks; and were surprised, indignant and embarrassed by them, and by America's immediate retaliation. At any rate, Kosygin left Hanoi without publicly committing himself to offers of equipment. And when the international Communist conference took place in Moscow on 1 March 1965, the Lao Dong party boycotted it.

The Americans, for their part, did not immediately jump from retaliation to escalation. Instead, they gave Hanoi a chance of avoiding further consequences of their attacks of 7 February. On 7 April, President Johnson, in a major speech at Johns Hopkins University, defined America's objective as 'the independence of South Vietnam, and its freedom from attack'. Declaring that the United States was searching for a peaceful settlement, he announced its readiness for 'unconditional discussions'. (Hostile commentators were quick to seize on the point that 'discussions', however 'unconditional', do not have the force of *negotiations*. But in January 1966, an American statement explained that the U.S. was ready for 'unconditional negotiations' and also, if Hanoi so preferred, for 'informal unconditional discussions'.)

On 8 April, Hanoi responded to President Johnson's Johns Hopkins speech with a statement of four points that would have to be recognized as the basis of a settlement before there could be any talk of a conference:

1. The United States must withdraw its troops, dismantle bases, end its military alliance with South Vietnam, stop intervention there and all acts of war against North Vietnam.

2. Pending peaceful reunification, both zones of Vietnam must bar foreign forces and avoid military alliances.

3. South Vietnamese affairs must be settled by the South Vietnamese *in accordance with the programme of the National Liberation Front*, without foreign intervention.

4. Reunification must be settled by the people of the two zones without foreign intervention.

It will be seen at a glance that the position of the two sides were totally incompatible, since the North Vietnamese were, in effect, calling on the Americans to stop defending South Vietnam and allow the National Liberation Front – an extension, as we have seen, of the North Vietnamese Communist party – to impose its views on the South Vietnamese. At this stage, then, the choice before President Johnson was between withdrawing from Vietnam (that is, conceding defeat); confining American aid to South Vietnam to advice and supplies (that is, allowing South Vietnam to be defeated sooner or later); and intervening more actively in an attempt to force North Vietnam to retreat from its extreme position. Since only the third course offered a chance to fulfil America's stated objective, this was the one President Johnson chose. In June 1965, he decided to authorize the use of American troops for combat (as distinct from defensive or advisory) duties; and the rapid build-up of the U.S. forces in South Vietnam ensued.

It is not my purpose to describe in any detail the various initiatives that have been made since then to bring about a negotiated settlement in Vietnam. The important thing is that all such moves – whether by Britain or other interested countries, by the United Nations or by the United States – have foundered on the rock of Hanoi's unwillingness to discuss anything at all until the Americans accept its 'four points'; that is, until they concede defeat. In contrast, the Americans have at all times been willing to discuss or negotiate with the North Vietnamese. Whether the peace moves were secret or open, Hanoi's attitude has remained intransigent. For instance, the mediation attempts by the UN's Secretary-General, U Thant, in March 1967, came to nothing; so did President Johnson's secret offer of talks a month earlier, in a letter to Ho Chi Minh, which Hanoi published and rejected on 21 March.

The point (as emerges from captured documents summarized in Part IV, 3) is that *Hanoi is not interested in negotiations*. Three possible developments could, however, change this attitude:

– If the Viet Cong established a clear military superiority over the South Vietnamese and Americans. In that event, negotiations would be offered, in order to secure maximum political advantages under international approval. While negotiations went on, military attacks would be intensified, so that the enemy's deteriorating position would force further concessions. This is what happened in Vietnam in 1954 and in Laos in 1961 and 1962, in both cases while the respective Geneva conferences on the country's political future were in progress.

—If the Viet Cong's military situation showed signs of gradual worsening. In that event, negotiations would serve the purpose of gaining some kind of *de facto* representation of the National Liberation Front. (If the worsening came suddenly, however, the Northern Regulars might well be withdrawn quietly, leaving the guerrillas and terrorists to carry on.)

—If American public opinion turned decisively against the war. Negotiations could then turn even an American military victory into a diplomatic defeat.

The last of these points is of great importance. One of the reasons why 'revolutionary' war can sometimes win superficially surprising victories against apparently overwhelming military odds is that a democratic country, caught in a rising spiral of expenditure and casualties, becomes increasingly vulnerable to the anti-war pressure of public opinion. In the end, this is why France lost the first Indo-China war, and later, the Algerian war (in which the French had established unquestioned military superiority). If the Americans are defeated in Vietnam (and by 'defeated' I mean forced to concede Hanoi's terms), it will not be by military means but because public support for the war, within the United States, will have dwindled to vanishing point.

The North Vietnamese Communists are, of course, well aware

of such realities; and so are Communist Parties all over the world, which – whatever their doctrinal differences – are all united in support of Hanoi and in hostility towards American intervention. It is this fact that provides the 'steam' behind the anti-American 'Teach-ins', anti-war demonstrations of all kinds, the Bertrand Russell 'trial' of the United States for alleged war crimes, anti-American advertisements in the Press, and similar manifestations. I do not for a moment mean to imply that all who support, or even all who sponsor, such campaigns, are Communists. Clearly many of them – probably a substantial majority – are genuine pacifists or people who, often for defensible reasons of their own, are against the American bombing of North Vietnam. Indeed, it is an essential part of these campaigns that most of the signatories or participants should be non-Communist or even non-political. (As Professor Hugh Trevor-Roper has wisely observed, a surprising number of them are scientists and mathematicians, whose knowledge of the issues is probably as profound as, for instance, is my knowledge of the quantum theory or the technique of nuclear fission.) The impulse, and very often a major part of the funds, however, are from Communist sources.

The scale of the 'quit Vietnam' campaign is as vast as the objective in sight: the defeat of the United States. It flourishes in every western country. The methods used are as unscrupulous as one might expect, and the organization is meticulous. To give only one example, when a British Labour M.P., Mr Alan Lee Williams, had a letter published in the London *Times* of 8 April 1967, supporting the American intervention, he received 700 hostile letters the following day; and for forty-eight hours, his telephone rang constantly with abusive or obscene calls.

The 'quit Vietnam' campaign is one of the realities of the crisis. Let us consider other realities:

ESCALATION

This is a two-way process. In the early stages of the second Indo-China war, the problems facing the South Vietnamese government were terrorism and guerrilla war. In time, the Viet Cong guerrillas started fighting in larger units. More and more regular army officers and more and more sophisticated weapons, many of Russian manufacture, came down from the North, either by way of the 'Ho Chi Minh trail' through Laos, or by sea. It is difficult to put a precise date on this gradual development; but the time came when two wars were found to be in progress instead of one. The 'little' war – terrorism and small-scale guerrilla operations – went on in the shadows. The 'big' war had started, too.

The 36,000 regulars and 80,000 irregulars on the Communist side grew until – by the autumn of 1966, the corresponding figures were 90,000 and 105,000. Of the 90,000 regulars, fighting in regiments and battalions, some 25,000 were North Vietnamese. In addition, there were about 40,000 technical and political cadres and 15,000 logistical support personnel – a grand total of 250,000 men. By the spring of 1967, this figure had probably risen to 300,000, mainly through further infiltrations from the North.

On the American side, the 16,000 or so advisers of pre-escalation days have been supplemented by combat troops in large numbers. By the autumn of 1966, there were about 330,000 American troops fighting in Vietnam. By the spring of 1967, the figure had reached 445,000; and by June 1968 it is expected to rise to 525,000, without counting the 50,000 seamen and airmen of the Seventh Fleet. Still on the American side, escalation has also meant an accelerated programme of construction of jet airfields and other military installations, and a massive programme of bombing, aimed at military objectives in North Vietnam.

In his speech before the U.S. Congress at the beginning of May 1967, the U.S. Commander-in-Chief in Vietnam, General William C. Westmoreland, described the accelerated construction programme in these words: 'Two years ago . . . there were three jet-capable runways in South Vietnam. Today there are fourteen. In April 1965, there were fifteen airfields that could take C-130 transport aircraft. We now have eighty-nine. Then, there was one deep water port of seagoing ships. Now there are seven.'

As for the bombing, perhaps the simplest way of conveying its scale is to state that during 1966, 300,000 tons of bombs were dropped on North Vietnam: the 1967 total which was not available when these lines were written, is considerably higher.

It would, however, be a grave mistake to suppose that the conflict has become a war between North Vietnam and the United States. True, the Americans now bear the brunt of the fighting. But with them are about 270,000 South Vietnamese regulars, 150,000 Popular Forces, 110,000 Regional Forces and 60,000 Police. On paper, these outnumber the Communist forces. In battle, the South Vietnamese are often outnumbered, for only 100,000 or so of their troops are in combat units; the remainder are lightly-armed static defence forces.

REGIONAL ALLIANCE

Nor do the Americans and South Vietnamese stand alone in the field. With them are 45,000 South Koreans, 8,000 Australians, 2,000 Filipinos and 540 New Zealanders. In addition, 1,000 Siamese troops were sent to South Vietnam in February 1967; at the end of the year the figure was rising to 10,000, this marked the first direct participation of Siam in the conflict. Indirectly, however, Siam had long been involved. Six large air bases have been built or expanded by the United States in Siam. In January 1967, there were 35,000 American troops in Siam, of whom 8,000 were engaged in construction work. On 9 March, it was officially confirmed that Siam-based American planes were bombing targets in North Vietnam; and by the end of the year, probably more than 50 per cent of such raids started from Siam.

What all this meant was that the formal alliance of SEATO, which had ceased to have much meaning, had yielded to a real alliance of East Asian and Pacific countries, the reality of which was proved by direct participation in the war. Without the need for a treaty, the fact of the alliance was underlined by a summit conference of the seven anti-Communist countries, held in Manila on 24-5 October 1966. President Johnson was there and so were the Presidents of the Philippines, South Korea and South Vietnam (Major-General Nguyen Van Thieu); and the Prime Ministers of Australia, New Zealand, Siam and

South Vietnam (Marshal Ky). The conference ended in a flurry of reciprocal pledges, which complemented the important statement of aims known as the Honolulu Declaration, and issued jointly by South Vietnam and the United States after a meeting between President Johnson, General Thieu and Marshal Ky on 7 and 8 February 1966. The hard core of the alliance – the U.S. and South Vietnam – was further cemented in March 1967 at a meeting in Guam between President Johnson and Marshal Ky.

THE STATE OF THE WAR

Within a few weeks of the American decision to send combat troops to Vietnam, it became apparent that the danger of military defeat in South Vietnam had been removed. The danger had been acute at the end of 1964, when talk of 'an American Dien Bien Phu' was heard. The change, once the decision had been taken, was dramatic.

To remove the fear of military defeat was not, however, to achieve the certainty of victory. For one thing, as I have pointed out, defeat may be inflicted in the public opinion polls and at the negotiating tables as effectively as on the battlefield. For another, there were two wars to be fought, and one was more efficiently prosecuted than the other.

Broadly speaking, the situation at the end of 1967 was that the big war was probably being won by the Americans, but the little war was not going as well as it might have for the Americans and South Vietnamese. At the end of January 1968, however, many facile assumptions on the Allied side were shattered by a massive and meticulously organized communist offensive.

Under the personal command of General Vo Nguyen Giap, the victor of Dien Bien Phu – who had secretly gone to South Vietnam for the purpose – Viet Cong irregulars, with a sprinkling of North Vietnamese officers, crept into half a dozen cities in small groups during the Têt festival, catching South Vietnamese soldiers and civilians off guard at a time of merry-making. Emerging fully armed in Saigon, Danang, Hué (the imperial capital) and other places, they attacked military and civilian

197

objectives, including the American embassy. In Hué, they seized the imperial palace, where they surrendered only after a 26-day siege. Meanwhile, at Khe Sanh, at the extreme west end of the 1954 demilitarized zone, some 7,000 American troops in an isolated fortress were surrounded by five or six times their own number of North Vietnamese troops in a situation reminiscent of the siege of Dien Bien Phu.

There was strong, though not absolutely conclusive evidence that the Communists wanted this to be *the* final offensive, designed to topple the South Vietnamese government and force the Americans to negotiate on Hanoi's terms. If so, the plan misfired. The Viet Cong guerrillas had been preceded by a series of broadcast calls to the local population to join in a general uprising. The uprising, however, manifestly failed to materialize. The guerrillas, apparently in anticipation of an uprising, had been told they would be relieved from the outside after 36 hours; but no relief forces arrived.

This is not to say that the offensive was in all respects a failure. Its success in the initial stages was a devastating demonstration of the ineffectiveness of South Vietnamese and American intelligence, since the Viet Cong plan could not have worked without a chain of complicity leading from the countryside into the towns. The discrediting of the Vietnamese administration was widespread, and this, too, was clearly one of the Communist aims.

On the other hand, the Viet Cong were shown to be unable to hold, as distinct from penetrating, the cities. Anticipating victory, they 'over-terrorized' the population: in Hué, for instance, they murdered 400 civilians, most of whom were later found in mass graves. Civilian casualties were indeed heavy, both from Allied fire and from Communist violence. It is probable that many civilians were included in grossly exaggerated figures of Communist casualties during the offensive, which I am therefore not quoting here. It is clear, however, that the Viet Cong paid a high price for such successes as they won. And in the end, morale within the South Vietnamese forces was higher than it had been for a long time, although indifference remained a major problem. But indifference is not the same as support for the Communists.

SOUTH VIETNAM

Why are the South Vietnamese indifferent? Why do the Vietnamese fight better on the Viet Cong side than on the government's? There are many answers to these important questions. One is that the South Vietnamese people have mostly known only aloof, despotic, inefficient or unjust government. This was true under the Diem family despotism, and also under the short-lived administrations that followed it until, in June 1965, the comparatively stable and enlightened military government of Thieu and Ky took over. To the Vietnamese peasant, in general, 'government' is an evil word. The fact that the Communists fight against the government – whatever government – is a passive point in their favour. Terrorized out of their indifference by the Viet Cong, and indoctrinated into accepting a programme whose merit they have no means of judging, they may at least feel they have something to fight for. When they defect – as they do – they know that death awaits them if they stay within reach of the Viet Cong. That is why so many more Viet Cong defectors than South Vietnamese army recruits cross the line to the other side, bringing with them intelligence of great value to the allies.

It should also be remembered that it is the Vietnamese peasants who bear the brunt of the fighting and suffering. In this context, land reform is of great importance. The various land reform schemes in South Vietnam, from Bao Dai's time to Nguyen Cao Ky's have yielded relatively little to the peasant. In contrast, the Viet Cong give land to individual peasants, as the Viet Minh did in North Vietnam. It goes without saying that the peasant is not warned that in time the land will be taken back from him and collectivized. A genuine and effective land distribution scheme, however costly, is therefore an essential ingredient of victory.

It has long ceased to be true, if it ever was, that the Americans suppose the war can be won by military means alone. The need for political and social action to win the little war is fully understood, and a whole terminology has grown up to express it. The big war, officially known as the 'main forces' war, is also called 'search-and-clear'. It is conducted by the Americans and their non-Vietnamese allies. The little war is conducted under the operations known as 'clear-and-hold' and 'hold-and-build'. The clear-and-hold tasks are allotted to the Vietnamese forces; the hold-and-build ones to 'Revolutionary Development Cadres' trained to work in the villages and help in various practical respects.

At this stage, two comments can be made about the state of the Revolutionary Development. One is that the Viet Cong fear it: during the first five months of 1967, 200 members of RD teams were murdered. The other is that unless the teams can be protected from the Viet Cong, the whole programme will prove useless. It should be added that, unfortunately, the 'search-and-clear' operations, often involving the destruction of villages with napalm, probably inhibited progress in the 'little war'. The effect of such operations on public opinion was also important. While they kept American casualties down, they played into the hands of those trying to prove the Americans guilty of 'war crimes'.

It can at least be said that since June 1965, South Vietnam has had a government which has gradually imposed its authority over dissident army officers and intriguing politicians, and even over the restless and powerful Buddhist groups which had contributed to Diem's downfall. It has survived more than one cabinet crisis. In the face of Viet Cong intimidation, it has successively, and successfully, weathered provincial Constituent Assembly, village council, Presidential and parliamentary elections. In particular, the Presidential elections of 3 September confirmed the Thieu–Ky team in office, with the former as President and the latter as Vice-President. Senate elections were held at the same time, and a new House of Representatives was elected on 22 October. To be sure, complaints of fraud at the polls were widespread, and it would be surprising if it had been otherwise, in a country with Vietnam's history. The important thing was that a reasonably effective team was given a chance to improve on its performance. And the extraordinary thing was that elections could take place at all, for it all happened against a background of continuing inflation – despite devaluation of the Vietnamese piastre – black marketing and widespread corruption. It should be added that neither inflation nor corruption is peculiar to South Vietnam.

NORTH VIETNAM

The American bombing has not put North Vietnam's extraordinarily efficient war machine out of action. But it has caused enormous damage, especially to communications – roads, railways and bridges. As soon as damage is caused, it is repaired, but this has meant diverting manpower from industry and agriculture, with resulting shortages. Rationing has had to be tightened and there is a flourishing black market. Prices of necessities have risen. More seriously, perhaps, North Vietnam is now utterly dependent on other countries – mainly Russia and China – for military equipment.

This dependence has important consequences. North Vietnam is on China's doorstep and regularity of supplies, whether of Russian or Chinese origin, is conditional on Chinese good will. (In fact, the Chinese have placed all manner of obstacles in the way of Soviet deliveries and frequently denigrated the quality of weapons from Russia; this obscures the fact that China can only supply light arms, whereas the Russians send MiG–21s and other advanced weapons.) The fact that North Vietnam needs both its major allies does, of course, enable Hanoi to play off one against the other. But it also creates problems. Broadly speaking, the Chinese want North Vietnam to fight on, regardless of losses and dangers; while the Russians, though they have some military personnel in North Vietnam, urge Hanoi to negotiate with the Americans.

There is one thing, apparently, on which advice from the Russians and Chinese coincides, though for different reasons: both allies are thought to be advising the North Vietnamese to abandon the big war and concentrate on the little war. The Chinese reason for this advice is that Peking does not consider the circumstances to be ripe for escalation to a big war. The Russians advise abandoning the big war because they fear the ultimate consequence – a nuclear clash with America.

It may well be asked: why do the North Vietnamese insist on carrying on with the 'main forces' war, since both their major allies are against it, and since their present course carries the risk of the total destruction of their half of Vietnam ?

The answer must be sought in the politics of the Lao Dong Party leadership. For the past eight to ten years, the war faction has been in the ascendant in Hanoi. It consists mainly of the First Secretary, Le Duan, and the Chinese-trained Truong Chinh. The political future of these men and their supporters is at stake. To climb down would mean admitting that they had been wrong for a decade. It would mean the end of their political, and perhaps their biological, lives. The main advocates of a scaled-down war are Vo Nguyen Giap, the Defence Minister and victor of Dien Bien Phu; and Pham Van Dong, the Premier. This does not mean that the little-war advocates are in favour of immediate negotiations; but they would presumably accept negotiations as a political weapon after a prolonged and success-ful subversion campaign in South Vietnam. While the Le Duan faction remains on top, however, Hanoi will not only reject all peace overtures, but do so stridently enough to satisfy the Chinese.

THE BOMBING

It is against this complex background that the American bombing of North Vietnam has to be considered. I am not concerned here with the morality of bombing; if I were, I should also have to consider the ethics of terrorism and of war in general.* What concerns us here is the *efficacy* of aerial bombing in the second Indo-China war. From this standpoint, the following conclusions emerge:

— *Communications.* The bombing has manifestly not pre-vented the flow of men and weapons from North to South Viet-nam. Indeed, the infiltration rate has increased. During the whole of 1965, a total of 150,000 North Vietnamese infiltrated into South Vietnam, in 1966, the total was 280,000. On the other hand, the flow of heavy weapons was severely handicapped. This much is certain: whenever a bombing truce has been in force,

* I have not changed the views I expressed on the relative morality of terrorism and bombing in *The Rebels* (Beacon Press, Boston, 1960), Part IV, 1.

the North Vietnamese have used it to step up their supplies. For instance, the truce during the Têt (Vietnamese New Year) was used to deliver supplies of the powerful 140 mm Soviet rocket from North to South. The verdict here must be that bombing is useful but not decisive.

— *Civilian morale.* By all accounts, it remains high under bombardment; as it did, for instance, in London under German bombing. Indeed, it has probably served to unite the North Vietnamese around their government.

— *Morale in the South.* The bombing of the North has undoubtedly raised the morale among all America's Vietnam allies.

— *Economy.* As we have seen, the economic damage is severe, whether in terms of damage caused or in diversion of manpower. This is a major part of the 'price of aggression' which, as President Johnson says, has been raised by the bombing.

— *Politics.* This, in terms of efficacy, is probably the best justification for the bombing. The longer the bombing goes on, the more the war faction of the Lao Dong Party's Politburo is open to criticism that it is exposing the Democratic Republic of Vietnam to total destruction for the sake of fighting a war which it cannot win. If this criticism forces the war faction out of power – and especially if the Chinese suspend supplies as a result and stop the passage of Soviet deliveries – the policy of bombing will have justified itself. It will not have justified itself if every building in North Vietnam is destroyed and the war goes on.

Essentially, this is a war of endurance. For the Americans, the Achilles heel could be the pressure of public opinion, especially if the war is still going on when the Presidential elections of 1968 draw near. Quite apart from the moral and humanitarian factors involved, the American voters may ask themselves whether it is worth $409,000 of their money as taxpayers for every Vietnamese Communist killed – the cost as calculated in April 1967.

Will the war faction in North Vietnam hold out that long? Much may depend on the answer to this question. If the war and the bombing are still in progress *after* the next American elections, whether under a Democratic or a Republican President, then the chances are high that Le Duan and his friends will be purged out of power.

It should be remembered, on the other hand, that even if the war faction is ousted, and even if negotiations start, the little war will not necessarily end. But the advantages of ending the 'main forces' war would be considerable. For one thing, it would enable the Americans and their South Vietnamese allies to concentrate all their efforts on ending the little war (thus emulating the feat of the British and Malayans, in relatively easier circumstances, in fighting off Communist terrorists between 1948 and 1960). For another, it would remove the dangers to world peace inherent in escalation.

In the second edition of this book, published early in 1966, I expressed the view that the dangers of escalation, though real, were exaggerated, in that the Sino-Soviet dispute made the circumstances uniquely favourable for American intervention. I still believe this to be true; and China's weakness during the 'cultural revolution' has strengthened me in this view. It remains that the longer the big war goes on, the greater is the danger of a major conflict, which could always happen if the Americans yielded to the temptation of invading North Vietnam.

Thus the long-term outcome of the war remains in doubt. An outright American 'victory' is in any case unlikely. If 'victory' comes, it will be because the North Vietnamese decide that the big war is too dangerous and costly; when the Viet Cong are isolated and reduced in numbers and when their politico-subversive apparatus has been destroyed. In these circumstances, the war will not end so much as fade away, as in Malaya and the Philippines. But one thing is certain: a negotiated peace that allowed the Viet Cong to gain a place in the Saigon government would mean defeat for the United States and the West as a whole – and, not least, for the Vietnamese people.

*

One more question should be dealt with: whether American intervention is justified on any grounds at all, and whether or not it is successful. It is argued, and not exclusively by Communists, that the Americans have no business in Vietnam and that it is of no particular importance, outside Vietnam, whether or not Ho Chi Minh wins.

It must be apparent from all that has gone before that I deeply disagree with such views. A victory for Vietnamese Communism would, in fact, have repercussions far beyond Vietnam's borders. Laos would be rapidly absorbed, and the threat to Cambodia and Siam would increase. More seriously, it has long been clear that Vietnam is a test case of the validity of Mao Tse-tung's theories of revolutionary war on a world scale. If Ho were allowed to win, Communist guerrillas and terrorists would draw their own conclusions elsewhere in Asia and as far afield as Africa and Latin America. If the world's most powerful country can be defeated in Vietnam, why not elsewhere ? If, on the other hand, it can be shown that revolutionary war does not pay, its advocates will be correspondingly disheartened. It could mean the end, to use Professor Walt Rostow's words, of 'the last great confrontation of the post-war era'. This alone would be worth fighting for.

As for the suggestion that the Americans have no business in Vietnam, or elsewhere in South-East Asia, one wonders whether those who make it have sufficiently pondered the implications. Either American responsibilities are world-wide, or they are limited to the western hemisphere. If the Americans quit Vietnam, they will not merely quit the Philippines and Okinawa as well; they will also, in time, pull out of Europe. If the European critics of President Johnson's policy are content to leave the defence of Europe to Britain's doubtfully independent deterrent and General de Gaulle's *force de frappe*, let them say so and face the consequences.

It ought to be hard for anybody with memories of appeasement in the thirties, American isolationism and Pearl Harbour, to preach a return to such disastrous policies. Yet this is the logical end of the critics' argument. Tragic though the plight of the Vietnamese people is, the Vietnamese crisis cannot be considered in isolation. It is, indeed, only a part of the world-wide strategic picture. An American retreat from Vietnam might bring peace – under Communist rule – to Vietnam and its neighbours. But in strategic terms, it would be a defeat of the first magnitude for the West as a whole.

Chapter Five PAX AMERICANA?

General de Gaulle may be right when he says that there is
no political reality in Asia that is not of interest and concern
to China. But it doesn't follow that China is in a position to
dictate the kind of order it would like to have in South-East
Asia. That time may come, but it is not yet in sight. It would,
in fact, be truer, and more relevant to present realities, to
say that there can be no settlement in Asia without America's
consent.

Some writers* speak of a decline of Western influence in Asia
and of an East resurgent. There is obviously some truth in this,
but here and now it is a very misleading picture. If 'the West'
means the British, French, and Dutch (with the Portuguese
where it applies), Western influence in East Asia is indeed on
the wane. But a phenomenon just as remarkable as the West
European withdrawal is often overlooked: there is now, on a
bigger scale than ever before, an American presence in East
Asia. The Americans occupied Japan and provided a liberal
framework for that country's astonishing economic achievements; they have a major base in Okinawa, which they are
treating as permanent, despite residual Japanese sovereignty;
they have bases in Formosa and the Philippines. They are

* For instance, C. Northcote Parkinson in *East and West* (Murray,
1964).

committed to victory in South Vietnam. And in the U.S. Seventh Fleet, they have one of the most awesome instruments of power in the contemporary world.

This reality of American power is the yardstick by which the various proposals for the neutralization of continental South-East Asia have to be measured. Prince Sihanouk has repeatedly called for the neutralization of that area, including his own Cambodia, and South Vietnam, but leaving out North Vietnam on the ground that it is already Communist and therefore 'committed'. General de Gaulle has several times proposed neutralization, but with studied vagueness. The first time was in a statement in Paris on 28 August 1963 in which he cryptically promised French help to Vietnam if it achieved 'independence' and 'unity'. The second time was in the General's press conference of 31 January 1964, in which he explained France's decision to recognize the Chinese People's Republic. The reference to China in the first sentence of this chapter was taken from that press conference, in which de Gaulle went on to mention – again cryptically – 'an eventual treaty of neutrality of the countries of South-East Asia'. Since then, one of his ministers has said neutralization would apply only to South Vietnam and another that it would include the North as well. The General returned to the theme in a strongly anti-American speech in Pnom Penh on 1 September 1966, in which he admitted that the Americans could not be militarily defeated but called for negotiations to prevent a world catastrophe.

In an ideal world, doubtless all small countries would be neutral and their more powerful neighbours would leave them in peace. But that is not the world as we know it. Any proposal for neutralizing Vietnam must be looked at in that light and must take account of the fact that North Vietnam is a Communist State with military designs on its neighbours. Prince Sihanouk is right when he says that you cannot easily neutralize North Vietnam; but wrong when he argues that you can neutralize South Vietnam alone. If the South alone were 'neutralized', the Americans would have to withdraw and the North would be left free to subvert the South at its ease. This is a non-starter.

Nor can Vietnam be united and neutralized by means of a coalition of Communists and anti-Communists, cohabiting under a neutral umbrella. This is the kind of government that was foisted on the Laotian people in 1962. It is not neutrality but chaos. Predictably, it soon broke down and the civil war resumed; and this is what would happen on a larger scale in Vietnam if the same 'solution' were tried there.

In fact, General de Gaulle's cryptic proposals make sense only on one assumption: that North Vietnam should be not so much neutralized as 'Titoized'. Titoization of North Vietnam was, in effect, what Jean Sainteny, the former French High Commissioner in Tonking, attempted in 1955 – after the first Indo-China war had ended – when he returned to Hanoi as Delegate-General. Sainteny's idea was to wean Ho Chi Minh away from dependence on either Russia or China, and offer him French aid and trade instead. It was not altogether a bad idea, but it rested on the assumption that North Vietnam would soon gain control of the whole country; and it collapsed because Ngo Dinh Diem, helped by his own courage and the Americans, stayed in power in South Vietnam.

When General de Gaulle made his statement on Vietnam in August 1963, Sainteny was a member of his cabinet, as Minister of Tourism and Veterans, and the General is believed to have consulted him before speaking. Clearly Sainteny's old plan was being revived.

The most logical outcome of the prolonged crisis in South Vietnam in fact seems to be – not the Pax Sinica or Pax Gallica proposed by de Gaulle, but a Pax Americana, with South Vietnam's independence guaranteed for as long as may be necessary by an American military presence and with North Vietnam made to realize that there is no future in subversion. Indeed, if this realization does dawn in Hanoi, there is no reason at all why North and South Vietnam should not co-exist peacefully and enter into normal trade arrangements under which the North would at least gain (legitimate) access to the South's rice.

The only alternative to a permanent American presence in Vietnam that would help to preserve peace would be the total demilitarization of the country, North and South. If this were done – and it would be far from easy – neutralization would make sense. Without it, neutralization would be a sinister farce. Indeed, in Vietnam and in Korea, the facts of power dictate an American presence, until such time as the Communist governments of East Asia have lost interest in subversion. This could well take more than a man's lifetime.

Indeed, any suggestion that there is a quick or easy solution to South-East Asia's problems would fly in the face of the facts as I have tried to outline them in the preceding pages. There is nothing tidy, comforting, or cosy about South-East Asia. Energies and resentments that were quiescent during the colonial period, or only occasionally palpable, are now in permanent ferment. National particularisms are being reasserted, often in a xenophobic form. The pressing problems of scarce food and more mouths are given less attention, by and large, than dreams of economic growth that, in many cases, seem likely to remain dreams because the measures taken to realize them have little relevance to the real problems that are faced. In this context, the 'socialism' professed by the majority of the countries in the area is an emotion rather than an economic theory – no less an emotion than the national mould into which each country's 'socialism' is forced. Such emotions are perhaps understandable: independence has come from a revolt against 'imperialism', and 'capitalism' is associated with 'imperialism' in nationalist minds. The phenomenon is by no means peculiar to South-East Asia, as a glance at the ideologies of emancipated Africa will show.

In time, perhaps, the connexion between private enterprise and affluence – so dramatically illustrated in Japan, and clear enough on a more modest scale in Malaysia – may displace the old and irrelevant association. (The creation, on 24 November 1966, of the Japan-backed Asian Development Bank was a hopeful step towards sanity.) But in the meantime, many years will have been wasted, while ill-trained and often corrupt administrations try to cope with matters better left to private firms. These will be dangerous years, for the fundamental problems will get worse, and the calm and peace that might encourage sane domestic and international policies seem unlikely to be forthcoming.

I have tried to show in these pages the interaction of the twin forces – Communism and nationalism – that have brought South-East Asia to its present state of turmoil, especially in Burma, Indo-China, and Indonesia. The whole region has travelled a long way since the relatively simple days of the 1920s, when all the countries of South-East Asia (except Siam) were colonies, and all the emergent Communist parties were in the last resort controlled from Moscow. Many things have blurred these relatively clear dividing lines: the struggles for independence; the emergence of sovereign nations; the nationalist tinge of Ho Chi Minh's Communism; more momentous still, the emergence of a national Communism in China; the Sino-Soviet split; the military presence of the United States; military dictatorship in Burma; the British-backed federal experiment in Malaysia and ex-President Sukarno's ambitions. These are the most important developments I have tried to describe. It needs no special gift of prophecy to say that they will continue to keep South-East Asia in a state of turmoil for many years. If the turmoil were merely local it could perhaps be complacently ignored in Western capitals. But it is not. South-East Asia has long been a battleground in an uncomfortably 'hot' cold war, and it could become, at any time – perhaps by the time this book appears – a battlefield of the great powers.

It is hardly the function of a book to prevent such disasters. I have written this one with a more modest aim: as a small and inevitably defective contribution to the understanding of a situation that affects us all more than we may care to admit.

SUGGESTIONS FOR FURTHER READING

The list of books on South-East Asia is growing fast. Here is a short descriptive selection of those most likely to interest readers in search of a more detailed treatment of certain aspects of the subject than they have found in this book:

Part One

A History of South-East Asia, by D. G. Hall (1964 revised edition, Macmillan). Monumental and authoritative.

Major Governments of Asia, edited by Kahin (Cornall, 1963), and *Governments and Politics of South-East Asia*, edited by McVey (Cornell, 1959). These two large books, by various authors, provide factual background and intelligent interpretation. The first covers China, Japan, India, Pakistan, and Indonesia; the second, more relevant to this study, ranges over Thailand, Burma, Indonesia, Malaya and Singapore, Vietnam, and the Philippines.

Part Two

Communism in South-East Asia, by J. H. Brimmel (O.U.P., 1961), is a massive and fascinating guide, covering nationalism as well as Communism. *The Revolution in South-East Asia*, by Victor Purcell (Thames & Hudson, 1962), though occasionally idiosyncratic, especially about Malaya, is a wonderfully concise reference book.

The Emancipation of French Indo-China, by J. D. Lancaster (O.U.P., 1961). This is the best book in English on contemporary Indo-China, elegant, quietly humorous, and accurate. *The Struggle for Indo-China*, by Ellen J. Hammer (Stanford, 1954), is also useful, especially for its American perspective.

Two illuminating accounts of Chinese and Vietnamese theories of revolutionary war are: *Mao Tse-tung on Guerrilla Warfare*, by Samuel B. Griffith, and *Communist Revolutionary Warfare*, by George K. Tanham (both Praeger, 1961). My own *The Rebels* (Chatto & Windus, 1960) deals with the South-East Asian insurrections in a wider context.

Part Three

Communist China and Asia, by Doak Barnett (Harper, 1960), gives a full account of the phases of Peking's diplomacy and deals with America's China policy.

The most engaging introduction to Laos and its politics is Sisouk Na Champassak's artless *Storm over Laos* (Praeger, 1961); an informed eyewitness account is Michael Field's *The Prevailing Wind* (Methuen, 1965).

The fullest account of the second Indo-China war is in *The Two Vietnams* (Pall Mall, 1963), by Bernard Fall, but Denis Warner's *The Last Confucian* (Penguin, 1964) gets closer to the heart of it.

Still the best and most readable survey of the problems SEATO was meant to deal with is the work of a Chatham House study group: *Collective Defence in South-East Asia* (O.U.P., 1956). A more up-to-date but less consistent study is *SEATO*, edited by George Modelski for the Australian National University (Cheshire, 1962).

Parts Four and Five

Of the many books on Indonesia, the two most readable are probably: *The Story of Indonesia*, by Louis Fischer (Hamish Hamilton, 1959), and *Rebels in Paradise*, an eye-witness account of the 1958 rebellion by James Mossman (Cape, 1961). For more academic surveys, see the Indonesian sections of the Cornell University books mentioned under Part One above. Arnold Brackman's *Indonesian Communism* (Praeger, 1963) is an absorbing and well-informed survey. For an excellent account of more recent events, see Tarzie Vittachi's *The Fall of Sukarno* (Mayflower Books, London, 1967).

Communism in North Vietnam, by P. J. Honey, of the School of Oriental and African Studies, London, sheds much light on Ho Chi Minh's republic and its relations with Moscow and Peking (Massachusetts Institute of Technology, 1963). Of the many studies in insurgency in South-East Asia, the best and the most succinct is Sir Robert Thompson's *Defeating Communist Insurgency* (Chatto & Windus, 1966); see also the symposium, *VIETNAM: Seen from East and West* (Pall Mall, 1967). The standard work on the organization and techniques of the National Liberation Front of South Vietnam is Douglas Pike's *Viet Cong* (M.I.T., 1966). A recent major work is by Dennis J. Duncanson, formerly of the Thompson Advisory Mission in Vietnam: *Government and Revolution in Vietnam* (O.U.P., 1968), which uniquely contributes to an understanding of the problem.

The indispensable handbook for Burma since independence is Hugh Tinker's *The Union of Burma* (3rd edition, O.U.P., 1961).

INDEX

213

Index

Index

Index

Index

Index

Index